house of belief

creating your personal style

house of *belief*

creating your personal style

KELEE KATILLAC

SALT LAKE CITY

First Edition
03 02 01 00   5 4 3 2 1

This book is published by
Gibbs Smith, Publisher
P.O. Box 667
Layton, Utah 84041

Orders: (1-800) 748-5439
Visit our web site at www.gibbs-smith.com

Edited by Gail Yngve
Designed by CN Design
Printed in China

The photographs in chapter two and on pages 20-21 and 32-33 are by and copyright © of Lisa Helfert. All other photographs are by and copyright © of Roy Inman

Library of Congress Cataloging-in-Publication Data

Katillac, Kelee

House of belief: creating your personal style / by Kelee Katillac.—1st ed.
p.cm.
ISBN 1-586805-074-1
1. Interior decoration—Psychological aspects. 2. Values. I. Title.

NK2113.K38 2000
747—dc21   99-046589

Cover: An interactive gallery of belief—hand-glazed walls, library paneling made from recycled doors, watercolor pillows, and a sofa designed by the author—are belief-evoking symbols of personal creativity.

Half-title Page: A ritual of belief: the Rowzees computer scan images of people who have influenced them in their creation of a belief-based wall hanging. The framework is a wood grill that can be purchased at any home center.

Title Page: This moderne drawing room features silk geometric pillows and luxe striped curtains in velvet and canvas sewn by Laura. The focal point of the couple's belief-based decorating is a wall hanging that represents people who have influenced them, including pop musician Pete Townsend, political theorist Edmunde Burke, writer George Orwell, and fifteenth-century artist Albrecht Durer.

Dedication Page: In their house of belief, Laura and Andy Rowzee hand made nearly every element. In the bedroom, Andy painted the abstract floorcloth, reupholstered the wing chair, and washed the walls with brilliant cobalt.

Table of Contents: One of Cathi Horton's favorite rituals of belief is to go "treasure hunting" at garage sales. "I love to find a castoff and turn it into something representative of who I am. What makes it about me? The magic of my creativity and imagination," she says. A worn-out tabletop—one of Cathi's found treasures—was resurfaced with her hand-painted tiles.

Dedicated to Steven, Joan, Jack, Jodi, Gail, and all the rest

who truly *believed*

contents

confessions
of an interior designer
laying the foundation for a house of belief

Long before I laid the foundation for the sturdiest house I ever built, my own house of belief, I spent many years trying to find it. The journey to that place of spiritual expression reads like a twentieth-century Odyssey.

Opposite: Rather than popular style, this salon expresses the author's meaningful personal ideas. In a wall-sized mural, belief in the unity of the arts, sciences, and spirituality is depicted by icons of each domain. An exhortation to find one's own icons—"Ancestors are to be chosen"—calls from the table skirt.

Above: Favorite literary works can inspire actions of belief-based decorating. The book Art & Physics by Leonard Schlain did so for the author. Art materials kept close at hand, such as these hand-mixed paints in science flasks, make spontaneous actions of creativity easier to accomplish.

My clients and I had run off course, and I was steering the ship. For a few years we were cast adrift, searching in vain for a place to call "home." Our ship, *The Style*, kept carrying us farther and farther away, grounding us on foreign lands. In the English countryside, we were chased down by fox-hunting hordes. In the Southwest, giant cacti loomed fiercely, and in a barren new land called "Contemporary," our spirits nearly froze to death.

Continually blown about by the prevailing design trade winds, we traveled far and wide. Magazines and oracles lured us farther from our destination with their siren's song, "Here is the look, the feel, the fashion, and the color of home; try it now!" And mirages of the perfect style appeared and vanished before our eyes. No matter how many times we set out anew, the course was always predictable. My early journal notes tell the tale:

As a fledgling interior designer fresh out of the nest, I have as many decorating ideas to express as any client will allow me. The first in-home meeting with Mr. and Mrs. Client dealt with space and fabrics and, of course, budget. It all seemed perfect and I glowed with anticipation. Naturally the wife had all the preferences as hubby sat close by wearing a tight skeptical grin, his hand firmly grasping his wallet.

A later entry, same subject:

Somehow or other we make it through meeting after meeting, finally opting for English country over the husband's preferred leather-and-glass contemporary. The wife usually gets her way despite my best

efforts to be fair and give him a vote. So, Mr. Client finds himself preparing to purchase a reproduction of a reproduction of a portrait of an eighteenth-century earl, which is guaranteed to put the "English" in the English-country look. This is the style of the moment, so no one thinks to suggest the preposterous nature of such an acquisition except me. I think, where is the truth in this? If this is what being a designer is about, I don't think I can keep this up. Help!

mutiny on ship

For awhile this is how it went with my clients, despite my growing uneasiness with a process that produced such an artificial product. I had always thought of myself as a person of integrity, yet I was caught in the midst of a career that on a spiritual level seemed to have none. Oh sure, the prices were as fair as I could make them. My products were not only on schedule, but ahead of it. And my client relationships were cordial, though, as often as not, upon delivery of the draperies or new sofa, clients were dissatisfied.

Journal entry:

The nights before deliveries or installations are now sleepless since I have come to believe that my client's expectations won't be met. Not because the curtains weren't constructed as my carefully drawn illustrations show, or the wrong color was chosen, or the products were late or deficient in any technical way. Everything seemed perfect. What's even more frightening is that though the client seemed pleased initially, I can count on a delayed reaction. The call will come within a few days, a sort of nebulous expression of discontent, having to do with a flaw on the hem of the lining, or a husband's confusion over the bill, or a criticism by a mother-in-law of the color of the paint. Woe to me and my English-country ulcer.

One week after a delivery:

I tried every kind of communication and service strategy I could to ease Mrs. Client's apparent discomfort with—with something! Even when, with magnifying glass in hand, a loose stitch could be found nowhere, and all the painted trim appeared to be utterly perfect, she looked troubled, and so her trouble is now mine. Together we have become chronically troubled deep in our spirits. I must find a new career!

As a professional interior designer I had done everything that was expected—at least what appeared to be expected. But it seemed there was something else going on—a little voice in the back of my mind and the client's—a covert operation of the subconscious. As it turned out, the trouble was no trouble at all. It was simply that creative and artistic impulses within my clients were finding their way to the surface but had no means of expression, resulting in a confusing set of thoughts and actions. In other words, deep inside they wanted to create a home for themselves but weren't consciously aware of their desire and didn't know how to make it happen. I was as in the dark as they were.

So, when faced with the product of an interior-design process that had denied their own personal creative spirit its expression, a new kind of discontent arose within my clients—one they could voice, and their voice emerged as a vague dissatisfaction. We have all felt it. At first, this inner tension is difficult to understand because we have been given so little information about it. We are unaccustomed to recognizing the voice of our creative spirit.

Opposite: Artwork evokes observations and affirmations; chalk is an apt medium for applying such thoughts to painted walls.

Right: A hand-colored pillow featuring a machine gearshift further reconciles art with science.

land in sight

Homes that say nothing of who we are—what we believe in and values that we aspire toward—are places of tumultuous spiritual discontent. By filling the space around us with benign objects—department-store clones with matching accessories to fill every nook and cranny—we lock ourselves into a gilded cage of fashion for which our creative spirits have no key.

Intuitively we know that all things in physical form have meaning and that to surround ourselves in the personal space of our homes with things that hold no meaning is like opening our house to strangers. My point is very well illustrated in the case of the English aristocrat reproduction painting. It seemed blatantly intended to appear as a long-lost family ancestor in an attempt to carry off an English country look.

When it comes to nurturing spiritual feelings, ascribing to an interior-design look will always fall short because when we substitute someone else's vision for our own, deep in our hearts we feel denied. Only we can decide what is meaningful for us. When we are faced with an empty room, we see the possibilities—a new page on which to write a great story filled with friendship, love, creativity, and learning.

slaves of design

In the typical approach to home decorating, beliefs and dreams are rarely considered. These hidden longings of the spirit have been given no voice, and there are no current cultural examples to show the way—only interior-design mandates. These rules, designed to control the look, are often confusing and contradictory: Don't mix styles; go for an eclectic mix; never mix stripes and florals; mix patterns liberally; dark paint makes a room look smaller; dark paint can make a small room look larger. The obscene notions imposed by the design industry actually deter personal growth: The paintings should match the furniture; family photos should be limited, and here is one of the most outrageous: Never put paperback books on your bookshelf. These kinds of restrictions subjugate the things homeowners feel very strongly about to the demands of interior design.

Opposite: Inspiration comes in many packages. The most inspiring icons of all can be those we know best. Images of family members and friends who have triumphed against the odds become reminders that we can do the same. Nurturing inspiration can be easily accomplished when it is ever present in our home environments as is the case in this artful arrangement.

How did most people come to be enslaved by the demands of the fashionable look? It started during the Victorian era—about 100 years ago—when industry and mass production were charging forward. The requirements of long days in the factory or on the assembly line quickly began to change the way life was lived. Personal energy that had formerly been used for creative pursuits in the home environment, such as furniture crafting or sewing, was now depleted by long days of monotonous work, all under the guise of making life easier and better. To some degree it did, but at a great cost.

On cue to meet the demands of the market it was fostering, savvy capitalists produced matching suites of furniture in uniform designs, or styles. The emergence of the fashionable look actually relied upon the fact that people no longer had the creative energy left to think and create for themselves, having been depleted by work outside the home.

Throughout this century, the growth of the interior-design industry has depended on the notion that consumers are creatively depleted. As the century unfolded and more women began to work outside the home, the problem increased. Most homeowners today have become so alienated from their natural creativity that many have forgotten it ever existed. Buying into this twentieth-century myth, many people feel they don't have the license to give artistry or craftsmanship a try.

Today it seems that the only means one has to experience creative expression is secondhand. Through the creativity of career designers and artists, many people hope to buy a little of it for themselves. For awhile most homeowners were placated with the product of another person's creative process, and the interior-design industry thrived on this. But once again many homeowners are beginning to feel the desire within themselves to make their homes an expression of who they are and what they believe and value. By reflecting back to the Victorian era, anyone can learn how to create his or her own "house of belief."

home at last

William Morris, visionary artist and philosopher of the Victorian era, predicted that the industrial and technical revolution would strip the world of its humanity. He envisioned a world made spiritually bankrupt by machines that robbed us of the opportunity to express our own creativity. Mass production, he predicted, would dehumanize society and make people hostage to precisely the kind of interior design and decoration that leave out the precious ingredients of artistry and creativity.

By considering just a few examples of twentieth-century-versus-Victorian life, it's easy to see why homeowners have forgotten how to create a house of belief for themselves. During the Victorian era, all levels of society were involved in the active creation of their home surroundings. While the working classes might have built their own homes, made furniture, or sewn curtains, the gentry, too, were involved in the creation of their homes. They routinely designed the structure to reflect a preferred historic period. The architecture of the house would often perpetuate the occupant's most cherished ideals. For example, ancient medieval designs were popular because they were

An interactive gallery of belief—hand-glazed walls, library paneling made from recycled doors, watercolor pillows, and a sofa designed by the author—features are belief-evoking symbols of personal creativity. A touch of whimsy is added with the handwritten message "Be a cool cat" chalked above the framed print.

A handmade folding screen has been heat-transferred with images of twentieth-century architecture, making a cozy corner uniquely the owner's.

thought to represent the romantic notions of chivalry and honor.

Much emphasis was also placed on communing with nature in the Victorian period, most readily expressed in gardens designed for soulful contemplation. Summer houses and gazebos in romantic styles were constructed as places for outdoor gatherings. Tropical observatories, complete with exotic birds and plant life, would often be built within the main house. This was not mere opulent materialism; rather, it was the unrestricted growth of personal creativity and belief-inspired vision.

In all ways, the Victorians were involved with their homes. It became an artistic expression of the life of the occupant. The focus centered around the hearth, a place where family and friends gathered. Music, dance, and dramas, produced by the family members themselves, were typical entertainment for gatherings and social events. Group activities such as baking, quilting, and needlepoint allowed them to share their creative expression.

Today, giant decorating outlets turn out assembly-line furniture and draperies. The interior focus of the house is often toward entertainment centers—spaces filled with computer-generated images, massive TV screens, and all sorts of interactive technology. Home building is often limited to selecting from a few design plans offered by a builder in compliance with neighborhood codes that place many homeowners all in identical boxes. Flawless expanses of chemically treated bluegrass provide an assembly-line look for these boxes, replacing imaginative gardens, once places of retreat that invited one to sit and visit, with cookie-cutter yards that do little to raise spirits or soothe the soul.

the ritual of belief

Morris had a proactive solution. He knew that even as the modern world intruded on our ability to create and nurture our spirits, it was possible to sustain ourselves through artistry and craftsmanship. Simply put, Morris incorporated beliefs, goals, values, and dreams into the home to create a visual affirmation of who the homeowner was, what he or she aspired to and treasured. Through belief-based decorating, spiritual thoughts are brought into physical form.

The Victorians used rituals of belief to empower themselves. For example, a quote may have been stenciled to the wall or sewn into a bed hanging as an affirming reminder. A personal icon could be carved into the mantelpiece as a symbol of a life well lived. Images of nature—animals and plant life—were popular design motifs for handmade wallpapers and fabrics, underscoring the unity of life and a responsibility to honor it.

Morris knew the primary step in spiritual renewal and creating a house of belief. His Arts and Crafts movement concentrated on making the home environment an interactive gallery of personal belief. From this concept sprung his well-known adage: "Have nothing in your houses that you do not know to be useful or believe to be beautiful." In this declaration of the influence of our surroundings, we are exhorted to have nothing within sight that will degrade the quality of our beliefs.

a house of belief

Within the safe space of our homes, we should surround ourselves with images that uplift our hearts and minds. Those things that we have made with our own hands, along with the artistic expression of others, are tactile reminders that we are capable of bringing beauty into our lives. A handmade quilt or a fine novel carries with it a sort of spiritual energy that can inspire us if we open our hearts to it. In this process of viewing decorating as more than just getting things (new carpet, sofa, and curtains), we work with what we already have—our values—and create more than just a new color scheme.

My clients have come from diverse life experiences and professions: housewives, nurses, corporate executives, physicians, accountants, people with limited budgets as well as many unconstrained by financial considerations. This process of belief-based decorating has unleashed creative and artistic powers for many of these people, often in unexpected ways. We began by shaping their home environments into places of inspiration and affirmation, and frequently it led to further expressions of creativity and artistry in their lives.

One corporate trainer now plays the guitar, a housewife designs and crafts jewelry, an engineer collaborates with an artist to create drawings of his favorite authors. Another young woman, newly married, used her sharpened creative instincts to fashion party-decorating centerpieces and cakes. One client designed a music studio from a spare room in her home so she could resume her childhood love of playing the piano. And a seventy-year-old gentleman discovered a hidden talent for calligraphy. He writes warm personal notes to friends and relatives. Inspired by a new room with an eighteenth-century writing table and a dislike for mass-produced greetings, he painstakingly creates something he loves in an atmosphere he almost unconsciously created to produce this work. His creativity has blossomed anew at seventy, and

his personal values guided his design choices and unfolded into a more enriching life.

My own home is a classic example of artistry as a ritual of belief. Inspiration is everywhere. The writings of Shakespeare, Jane Austen, William Blake, D. H. Lawrence, Descartes, Einstein, and hundreds of others teeter in stacks on every table and chair. A giant mural weaves together ideas from these writers and stretches across one wall, bringing art and science together in a harmonious allegory, which provides great comfort to me in coping with this science-lab of a world.

Music of all kinds can be heard within my walls. One day, while listening to a Gregorian chant, I was inspired to plaster the wall trim in my living room and carve into it an archaic border pattern. As the chant breathed on, I felt myself easing into the spiritual rhythm of the Greek key pattern I was crafting. Unstuck in time, I glimpsed an ancient cathedral as I was transported by the power of the music. That moment is now captured in the walls of my home.

Photographs, letters, and postcards from those I care about are tacked magpie-like all around. Buttons from my grandmother's collection are nestled on a Wedgwood plate. Found objects of interest—vintage textiles, old pottery, and religious carvings—share space with paint and brushes, canvas, watercolor markers, rubber stamps, and sketch pads. An easel stands propped in the corner next to a 1930s tattered velvet sofa, laden with antique pillows and slung over with a cobalt blue Persian rug. This is not just an art studio; this is the "living" room of my home.

Value statements: an antique silk pillow displays old-world craftsmanship; a photograph of James Joyce suggests the power of the pen; a rose in bloom denotes natural creativity; and a Venetian vase represents travel abroad.

your ritual of belief

In a notebook, begin to assess your beliefs and values. These will be the materials for the foundation of your house of belief.

Make two lists. Entitle the first one "Beliefs" and the second "Values." The lists should include the things you hold deep in your heart. These may be broad concepts or specific things or goals. They are your most cherished ideas—the way you want your world to be.

Taking the first step is always the hardest. Once you begin this exercise you will be amazed at your ideas and how confident you feel.

Here are some statements to help you get started:

beliefs

I love _____

I believe in _____

If I could change the world, I would _____

My life is _____

values

My number one priority is _____

I value _____ above all.

The important people in my life are _____

My best characteristics are _____

Home is _____

If I could be anything, I would be _____

When I am out in the world, it is hard to believe in

_____

My heroes are _____ ,

because _____

If I could go anywhere, I would go to _____

If I could _____ all day, I would.

My favorite quote/book/movie: _____

When I see/do _____ , I feel more optimistic.

Note: Your lists should not be limited to answering these questions. These are merely a few examples to get you started. This list will never be finished. It will always grow and change as you do. You should keep it handy at all times—especially when you need a lift to remind you of who you are, which is what creating a house of belief is really all about. Have fun with this. It is not about anything but you and your beliefs and values. There are no wrong answers. Enjoy creating a new life and a new home for yourself.

Taken as a whole, my home is like an animated Victorian shadow box. It is a small world—interdependent and completely natural. The found objects of inspiration—bits of lovely fabric, seashells, and Celtic carvings—blur with their offspring artistic expressions. Paintings and plaster ornaments surround me with affirmations of my creativity. Who I am and what I believe and value are the very stones of my home's foundation.

When we are motivated by belief we can do anything. Belief built the Egyptian pyramids, the Great Wall of China, and St. Peter's Basilica. By keeping our beliefs in front of us in our homes and by building our belief and our confidence through artistry in our own homes, we enter into an exhilarating process that affects our lives on every level.

exercising the concepts

It is important to keep in mind that a ritual of belief is a belief plus physical action. A ritual of belief always ends in a positive physical form. Form is an object or expression that can be seen or touched. For example, a painting of a family portrait is a form. A letter to a friend is a form, as is a handmade quilt. Form takes creative ideas and makes them visible.

Walk through your house now and look for things that exemplify something of your beliefs and values. List objects and areas that have special meaning for you.

Take specific note of objects that are handmade and of heirloom quality. Also note photographs, books, and music-related items. Objects need not necessarily be antique to have value. New objects can certainly represent meaning to us. Look for objects that are 100-percent natural or made of recycled materials, representing a love of nature and a respect for the environment (if this is one of your values). Through this process you may be reminded of some values you have forgotten to put on the list. Go ahead and list them. For example, as you walk through your house, you may find that there are a number of floral patterns, maybe a picture of a garden, and several flower vases. This observation may make you aware of something that you were unconscious of before now: how much you love and value spring and flowers. This is a legitimate and powerful ideal in your life. Write it on the list and keep looking for more.

You will begin to view objects as representative of some meaning. This meaning may only be known to you—more of an association. In the description of my house, if you recall, there is a plate of buttons from my grandmother's collection. To anyone else they are simply buttons, but to me they are my childhood with my grandmother. Note the value or the belief represented in objects in your home.

On your list from part one, look for things in your home that represent your beliefs and values. Write the objects on the list beside their associated idea.

You may also see many things in your home that have no meaning to you whatsoever. (Sounds like a good time for a garage sale.)

the *church*
of the home

rituals of belief

We all need something to believe in, something good, beautiful, or true. If only we could find a concept so inspiring that we'd march headlong into life, convinced of our purpose and radiating belief, our story meant for stained glass.

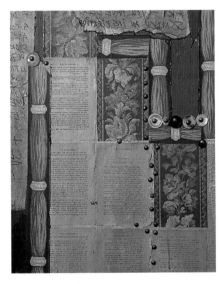

Opposite: As a healing ritual of belief, cancer survivor Geraldine Lloyd utilized bits of cutout wallpaper, antique lace, buttons, broken tile, written phrases, and torn book pages to form a wall collage of personal epiphanies.

Above: Pages from a book on unrequited love serve as a reminder of the importance of one's own life—even when a love affair has ended.

If only we could live nobly, walking a spiritual path, certain of our own special potential. If only we could find the means to live above modern skepticism that can ice our hearts, keeping our spirits from the life-giving movement of belief.

At times a walk through nature or perhaps a night sky showered by meteors can make us feel as though we have glimpsed something transcendent. The birth of a child can give us a sense of the creative continuum of life. A romantic scene in a movie reaches out to us, convincing us that we speak the same language of the heart. A midnight service on Christmas Eve rekindles our desire for the mystical, filling us with childlike wonder. At these times all the elements have lined up just right, our attitudes and the atmosphere, to help us sense the good, the true, the beautiful. For a moment our belief comes to life and the ice melts a little around our hearts.

Through these experiences, our ability to believe is increased. When we have an experience that illustrates our spiritual hopes in physical form, we feel as though those hopes have been fulfilled, that which we were longing to believe in has been proven to be true. We have seen it with our own eyes. The overjoyed heart says, "Yes! I was right. There is something greater than our own small planet, or life does go on, or I do have a soul mate!" This is how an idea becomes a belief. We have seen it in visible form; therefore, we can believe in it.

signs of belief

I think most of us have said at least once in our lives, "I'll believe it when I see it!" This simple statement briefly encapsulates the premise of belief-based decorating. When we represent our beliefs, values, goals, and dreams around us within our homes, we more easily accept them as truth. When we give life to these uplifting ideas by the process of artistic creation, they are no longer abstract concepts within our minds. They now concretely exist in the visible physical world. This action of bringing a good thought into physical form is a ritual of belief.

We don't correlate the inherent symbolism of the carved Egyptian figurine upon the mantel with an expression of our own beliefs. This little statue that was once a powerful symbol of the afterlife to the ancients has now become just an accessory to match our decor. The object has become separated from its spirit much the same way we have. We need to understand the meaning in things and why we choose them. By opening our minds to "see" the meaning in the materials from which our homes are made, we can begin to create homes that are designed by belief. In all things material, there is an essence of the spiritual.

This lost idea—that all things have a spiritual reference—now makes for a stunning revelation in our modern life. Most decorative elements throughout history, from color schemes to border patterns, came into being as an expression of a belief held by an individual or group, springing up out of mythologies, political systems, religious traditions, and everyday experiences. Old-world people expressed ideas that inspired them through their own special language of artistry. Signs and symbols were the language of the spirit. For example, a pattern of running ivy expressed eternal life, a golden key represented spiritual knowledge, and a dolphin indicated divine direction. Kings and emperors also cultivated their own lexicon of images: the laurel wreath represented honor, a running horse suggested liberty or freedom, and an eagle meant military strength. Color combinations in fabric and paints could also have symbolic meanings: earth tones of maize gold and celery green indicated a desire for a bountiful harvest, turquoise meant rain, and ivory with sky blue was for spiritual piety. These images are still with us today, though their meanings have become lost.

houses of worship

From ancient times, symbolic ideas were widely used in the decorative arts to create an atmosphere of meaning and purpose. Houses of worship have always relied on belief-based decorating to help create a spiritual feeling. This feeling was evoked through a collusion of sensory elements: space, color, light, sound, and smell. Art, architecture, signs and symbols, stained glass, statuary, paintings, and mosaics in natural materials such as

Within the aging framework of a fireplace mantel, Lloyd wrote a spontaneous poem. She said, "I just grabbed a brush and started painting in the words; it's amazing what God will do through us if we allow it." A sanctuary of creative and spiritual expression, her home is similar to a great cathedral where she works like a medieval artisan expressing a divine message.

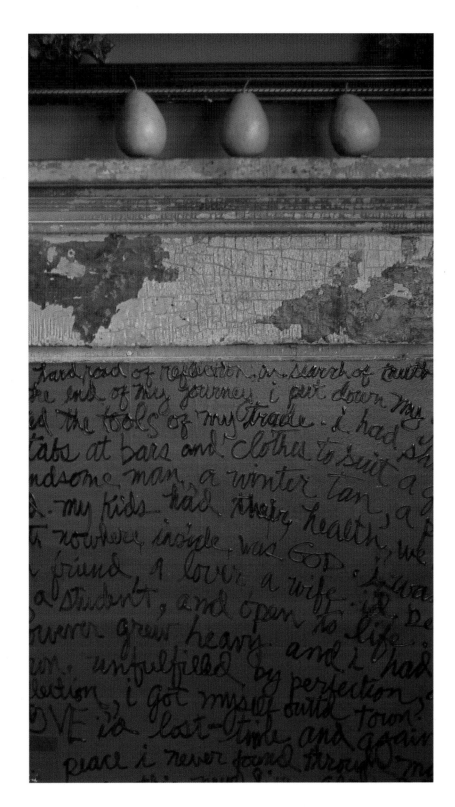

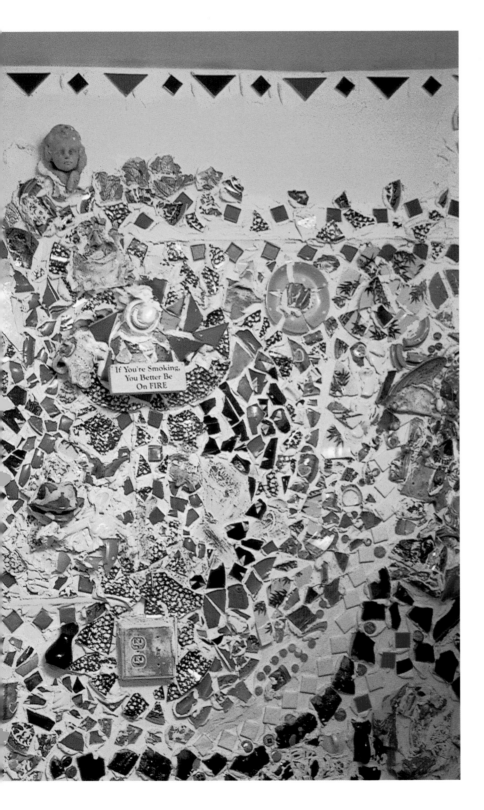

"Geraldine's kitchen": A ritual of belief: artist Geraldine Lloyd sees the beauty in broken fragments. Plates, knickknacks, seashells, and bottles were viewed as small pieces of life that had become misunderstood and castoff. Her ritual of belief reunited them into a meaningful wall mosaic.

marble and wood created the right combination of elements to help focus belief and inspire greater spiritual receptivity.

During Victorian times, church attendance was more pervasive than today. People were accustomed to seeing the use of artistry as a mode of spiritual expression. The grand old places of worship were the very embodiment of belief.

Up through the nineteenth century to the beginning of our modern age, belief-based decorating was practiced not only in the church but also in the home. It wasn't as if Victorian houses were laden with religious icons and scriptural verses. Victorians did, however, follow the examples of artistry and craftsmanship found in their churches to represent their own cherished ideas. Morris's Arts and Crafts movement considered the medieval church a model to be sought after, expounding on the quality and symbolism found there. Copying the art forms of the medieval church, Morris and his followers created their own art forms, such as allegorical tapestries and weavings, inventing their own personal symbolism to represent their beliefs and ideals.

In this manner, Victorian homes became houses of belief. Using the church as a visual outline for creating their homes, they used the same kind of art forms but varied the subject matter. For example, in the subject of a mural, they exchanged biblical stories for their own family story; for a phrase over a doorway, a Latin liturgy was traded for a Shakespearean quote; for tabletops, souvenir boxes were preferred to saintly relics; and for meaningful furniture, a sacred hand-carved wedding chest replaced the altar.

However, not all of their creative expression was derived from churches. Much of it was not even remotely sacred in the religious sense, although personal beliefs and values were still the true inspiration.

A few inventions of art and craft illustrated this point: leaves and trees represented in rolled-paper pictures showed a love of nature. A hand-crafted, trimmed, and tasseled cushion bestowed on the family pet demonstrated a love of animals; and a travel room, complete with exotic details, expressed a love of travel and foreign lands.

Creative expression seemed as natural as breathing to these people, and, really, for the spirit, creativity is as important as breathing. The Victorians benefited by the example shown them through church artistry. Art must have seemed a requisite of a growing spiritual life. It seemed vital for them to artistically express their beliefs, both spiritual and secular. As a result they were sure, even fervent, in their beliefs. This zeal, or positive life view, motivated them to express their ideas artistically without self-consciousness. Belief was the cause—art the effect.

visual affirmations

Today most of us don't go to church as often as people in earlier times. What's more, many of us don't find the same sense of wonder we felt in the religion of our childhood or any inspiration in the decorations of the buildings. Part of the reason is that many of our modern churches have been designed in the minimalist fashion, which can feel empty and coldhearted. It seems ironic that in a time when we need visual affirmations the most—to balance the negativity of the outside world—our contemporary churches and temples offer so little.

Not long ago I traveled to Notre Dame Cathedral in Paris. The journey through the streets of Paris to reach the church was quite a review of all the things that try our beliefs at the end of the twentieth century—traffic exhaust, gaudy billboards and advertising, and people exchanging less than friendly words and gestures. Newsstands announced a nuclear weapons inspection and the latest political scandal (and it didn't sound any better in "romantic" French). And there, just outside the doors of Notre Dame, a vendor tried to sell me a plastic replica of a long-forgotten saint. At that moment, I was tempted to join the unfriendly throngs, complete with internationally understood hand gestures. My belief in good, truth, and beauty was waning until I stepped from the harshness of the outside world, from the glare and confusion, through those big carved wooden doors.

It was as if I had stepped inside myself, somewhere close to my heart. The interior twilight engulfed me like a meditation. Moving forward in my own silent processional, I remembered the Victorian August Pugin's description:

Ideas in action: compelling words, such as believe, question, persevere, and observe, make each step a ritual of belief. Having the ritual in plain sight—as Geraldine Lloyd has done here on her staircase—so that it is repeated on a daily basis, or each time one climbs the steps, reinforces its impact.

It is, indeed, a sacred place; and well does the fabric bespeak its destined purpose: the eye is carried up and lost in the height of the vaulting . . . the rich varied hues of the stained windows, the modulated light, the gleam of the tapers, the richness of the altars, . . . all alike conspire to fill the mind [and spirit] with veneration of the place.

As Pugin mentions, the vaulting, the very architecture of the place—the great church in its physical form—suggests man embracing God. The central hall, or nave, with its right and left wings, forms the shape of a human body with torso and arms stretched outward—arms open to receive divine inspiration, baring the soul to receive the secrets of creation. Like priests performing a transforming ritual, the craftsmen forged their beliefs into works of artistry. Wood and stone were transformed into a body of belief with a rib cage of great buttresses, leglike pillars, and a heart of carved altars. All around me were materials from the outside world, that profane place from which I had just escaped, restored and transformed by human hands. I could see, yes, see evidence of God, not as remote or detached but as present and active, communing with man in a sort of divine collaboration.

I was illuminated by backlit broken color falling from the great stained-glass windows. As the rose, emerald, and topaz baptized me in an unearthly light, I felt the limitless possibilities of the creative spirit. I gazed up at the stories written in glass, though many of them I didn't know. They spoke truths that knew no time or place. Their message was one of the power of artistry to express beliefs and invoke the divine feeling in us.

Although the images, people, signs, and symbols that were portrayed in the decorations of the

Opposite: "As I began to get well, my rooms became lighter, brighter, and even whimsical," Geraldine said. In this second-floor sitting room, her sense of whimsy takes form in a Mad Hatter chandelier.

Right: In an autobiographical painting called The Empty Nest, *Lloyd applied photos of her children to the figure's weeping eyes.*

church may bear no direct relevance to me in my current life, they had deep meaning to the artisans who created them. And onlookers like myself may experience them as guideposts in their own spiritual journey, as exhortations "to be spiritual, to commune with the creator, to simply create!" There in the brushstrokes of a mural and in the deep carvings of marble statuary I could see something of God's own creative nature as it has been emulated through artistic expression. Art is God made visible.

reminding me of my own divine creative potential. I wanted to feel like this forever—creative and empowered.

artist as spiritual teacher

By creating our own houses of belief, we can live in an empowering atmosphere of self-expression. By bringing our beliefs into view, we can more easily remember them, even when we are chal-

It was a Sunday morning when I visited Notre Dame, and mass was in progress. What I felt that day defies religious classification. This was about the spirit—individual and unique. All around me this art of belief was communicating with me. Color, shadow, harmony, and phrase became sacraments that stirred my spirit,

lenged by the intrusions and skepticism of the outside world. The beliefs become an integral part of our realities when constantly in sight. Further, we can create an environment that encourages growth in all areas of life. Often, I have seen family, career, education, relationships, and health benefit from living in such an uplifting environment.

First, we must begin to think in terms of how to adapt belief-based decorating to our modern homes and lives. To do so we must look for guidance. In the days of the great churches, the artisans taught a valuable spiritual lesson through the ritual of belief: They allowed their convictions to move them into action, transforming their beliefs into art forms. As much as any priest or religious minister can teach us ideas about spirituality, so too can the artist, because, as we have seen, there is no greater means of becoming spiritual than through creative activity. The Victorians benefited from the influence of sacred art, and we can do the same by observing how a contemporary artist has created her own house of belief.

When artist Geraldine Lloyd bought her early-1900s house, it had been broken apart by the experiences of its life. What was once an elegant Victorian structure of architectural unity had been subdivided into three apartments; walls, like fissures, kept it from wholeness. As Geraldine looked upon the house, she could see an image of her own life, which had also been shattered into three pieces of experience. There was her earlier life as a wife of an important public figure, which ended in a painful divorce; her successful career as a mixed-media artist; and her present condition as a post-op throat cancer survivor. In the process of restoring the grand old mansion to wholeness, Geraldine found a means of restoring herself.

When I would get fixated on negative things about myself, knowing I couldn't eat and recognizing the limits of my life, I would get up and get going. I would use whatever paint I had, whatever materials I

Affirmation pillows and an antique patchwork quilt make the bedroom a nurturing retreat. "I love to make my illustrated journal books here—it feels safe,"Lloyd said. The artwork above the bed adds to the sense of well-being.

had, and begin to decorate and create and paint and build. This house really embraced me.

Not only did the radical laryngectomy, which removed a tumor from her voice box, leave her unable to eat but also unable to speak. She cannot paint and talk at the same time, because to talk she must press the button on her throat microphone. But, within this interactive art form of her home, she has found both sustaining food and a voice with which to express herself. This is the food and language of the spirit.

As an artist, and one familiar with that intuitive voice of the creative spirit within, she works spontaneously, using art as a process for her healing. Like her life, her home is a work in progress. Yet, already there are empowering sculptures, paintings, and quotes decorating even the most out-of-the-way spaces. Walking from room to room, her story unfolds like a 3-D mural, like those mystical dioramas found in the great cathedrals and temples. In small tableaux made from unexpected materials, unexpected revelations take form.

In reference to her divorce after many years of marriage, there is a library wallpapered with pages from a book called *Unrequited Love*. The tale of a foolish young woman who pined for love unfolds page by page in rows from floor to ceiling. "I started reading it and realized how stupid it was to ruin your life over another person. So I began ripping out pages and pasting them to the wall. Chapter 1 is right there by the door." To Geraldine, it's a reminder of the importance of one's own life and especially one's own self-esteem.

In another room is a large painting of a woman in tears. The tears are seemingly composed of memories, as tiny photographs of Geraldine's children form a collage inside the woman's eyes. "I call it my *Empty Nest Painting*," explains Lloyd.

Some of the works in the space serve as cathartic expressions of her life experiences, summing up and liberating at the same time. Others are uplifting statements of belief. High up in her second-floor hallway is a morning sky in perpetual sunrise, painted as an optimistic statement about the future. Painted on the wall below is a picket fence, burnished with gold and leading to an altar complete with a goddess figure. Very often, Lloyd chooses a goddess image to represent positive aspects of herself.

In her dining room she offers a feast of possibilities. Over crimson walls she has fixed bits of mirror broken into mosaic pieces. The effect is that of many perspectives. "So all who eat here will see each other in a new way," she says.

The old, the cast-off, the used-up—once again, all bloom to life within this artist's life-giving belief in the power of art. Her kitchen has become a kind of mystical place of transformation, aptly enough because the mixing of food substances in cooking is one of our most common forms of alchemy. But this has to do with visual alchemy. Broken plates, bottle tops, odd knick-knacks, glass wings, and seashells are embedded into rough plasterlike stucco, making the space feel like a little monastic grotto. Stained glass is even hinted at as she has wedged colored bottles into a window frame.

All through the house Geraldine has performed artistic rituals of transformation. Old objects take on new life. Old experiences gain new perspective. What many people would deem

Right: A Book of Belief catalogs personal beliefs, values, goals, and dreams and then becomes a resource for ideas and images to use in belief-based decorating. This particular book includes buttons and old photographs.

"beyond hope" she has found redeemable—from a broken plate to a broken body. Even old drawers have found use as a bookcase in her living room. And now Geraldine plans to open her home to other women who are struggling to heal their bodies and spirits. "This house has helped me to heal, and I want to open it to other women facing similar diagnoses and surgeries. The women would bring their personal effects and a good pair of shoes, and I'd offer them a chance to find themselves—through art, textiles, music, painting."

belief + action = ritual

In traditional houses of worship, rituals like communion, baptisms, or bat mitzvahs and bar mitzvahs are employed to help absorb the teachings into one's own spirit. Rituals are a constructive use of spiritual ideas joined with physical actions. The intent is to transform or move us from one place to another. In her own home, Geraldine Lloyd used the artistic ritual of belief to move her forward by reinforcing her positive ideas. Through the ritual of her artwork her beliefs are put into action.

Creativity is to the spirit what blood is to the body, and when we are spiritually depleted only a transfusion that is creative in nature will restore us. Working in her own small chapel, like a priest of artistry, Geraldine has used a similar approach to that of old-world artisans. The comparisons are numerous:

the structure
Houses of worship: Medieval cathedrals were designed in the shape of a human body.
Geraldine's house: In its broken state, it is reflective of her own wounded body.

field trip

Think about churches, temples, or other atmospheres that have inspired you. Art galleries and museums of antiquity are ideal, as well as old government buildings. Go visit one. Typically, the older the structure, the better. Older-style buildings are richer in the ornamentation you want to observe for this exercise. You need a vocabulary for your beliefs.

Once you have a place in mind, visit it and focus primarily on the artistry and craftsmanship that have been used to express ideas and beliefs. Look at the images and symbols. You may not understand at first what ideas the symbols are meant to represent. That's okay. However, you have chosen your site because something about it inspired you. Let's discover what it is so you can include it in your personal language. Just as a child begins to speak by listening and imitating, you are going to "listen" to the language of the artists who have created your site. Use books and magazines to help you. You may already have a guidebook for your site. If not, ask for or find one.

You may also use general resource guides, such as pictorial guides on Gothic cathedrals and Orthodox synagogues. One valuable book is *The History of Art* by Jansen. Most bookstores that carry art and design books also have a guide to signs and symbols, which would also be valuable.

As you tour your site, take plenty of time. You may want to make several visits. Look closely at the stained-glass windows, paintings, statues, wood and stone carvings, altars, tile mosaics, benches—any aspect of ornament, no matter how small. Observe the detail in the large works. Again, even though you may not know the story or characters of the beliefs, try to guess what idea(s) they represent—a story of creation or a nature scene.

the story

Houses of worship: Religious images from sculpture to mural tell a mixed-media story of the tenets of the faith.

Geraldine's house: Tall mannequins stand like actors in a passion play, photographic groupings compose visual chapters, and affirmative quotes write a narrative of her life.

the forms

Houses of worship: Stained glass; mosaic pictures; signs and symbols carved in relief; handmade psalters (or prayer books); ceremonial furniture such as altars, prayer benches, and confessional booths; and ritual objects like incense burners, candelabras, and chalices are all representations of a belief in a physical form.

Geraldine's house: All through her house of belief Geraldine has used fragmented bits of glass, mirror, and pottery to imply mosaic forms. Love letters, like small books of inspiration, are displayed prominently. She has created an altar to remind herself of her own divine attributes. It includes a heavenly sunrise that promises good things to come. And a room papered with book pages acts as a small confessional in which she liberates herself from past injuries.

getting started

Although church art generally illustrates religious ideas, in our homes we can express any idea that uplifts and empowers us. Whether it is about interests like travel, literature, or music, or about values like family, friends, and sharing, any idea that helps us to believe is a good one. For example, one of my clients had long been involved in Native American activities. She found herself attracted to their way of life and spiritual views. She represented this in her home by hand-painting her floor with good-luck signs from American Indian lore. She then painted phrases, such as blessings, over every doorway. They say, "Trust," "Believe," "Create," and "Love."

Another young couple emblazoned the quotation "The ornaments of a house are the friends who frequent it" across their fireplace mantel. This is a statement of their value of friendship. Above the mantel they hung antique black-and-white photographs, newly framed in bright red, of their parents in their youth. Also, to remind themselves of their own rural upbringing, they commissioned an artist to paint a colorful mural of small-town life.

We may find it difficult at first to identify what motivates us because we have grown unaccustomed to looking for meaning and symbolism in these modern times. Our contemplative side is slumbering. But by using the same process that has benefited my clients, we all can awaken our creative spirits and learn to decorate meaningfully in our houses of belief. The following exercise will help.

exercising the concepts

In the previous chapter, we made a list of beliefs and values in our very first ritual of belief. Now, we should take out those lists and begin to find images that represent the items on the list and speak personally to us. For example, if we listed love as a value, we might choose to represent love by deciding what it means to us. The love of family and friends might be represented by strategically placed photographs of these loved ones in plain view. Or, if we listed creativity as a value, we might choose to represent it with images of those artists that have influenced us most.

your ritual of belief
part one

Begin to create your own sourcebook or collection of images and quotes that will inspire you in making a house of belief.

First, look over the two lists you created in your first ritual of belief in the previous chapter. Beside each idea, note a visual symbol that might represent that belief or dream. These needn't be elaborate or complex; they need only speak to you. For example:

Positive Belief—friendship

Representing Image—a handshake, photograph of friend, or an embrace.

Cherished Value—travel

Representing Image—a boat on water, exotic places, or a mountain climber.

Use your imagination to represent your spiritual idea in a visual context. There are no wrong answers. What speaks to you? What represents your idea?

part two

Using a small notebook or loose-leaf binder, begin to paste cutout, drawn, or fabricated images that represent those you have noted on your belief and value list. Newspapers and magazines or your own drawings and photos are good materials to use. Also, inspiring quotes or uplifting cards and letters can be included in your book of belief. (Note: A small book allows you to carry your beliefs in your handbag or briefcase.)

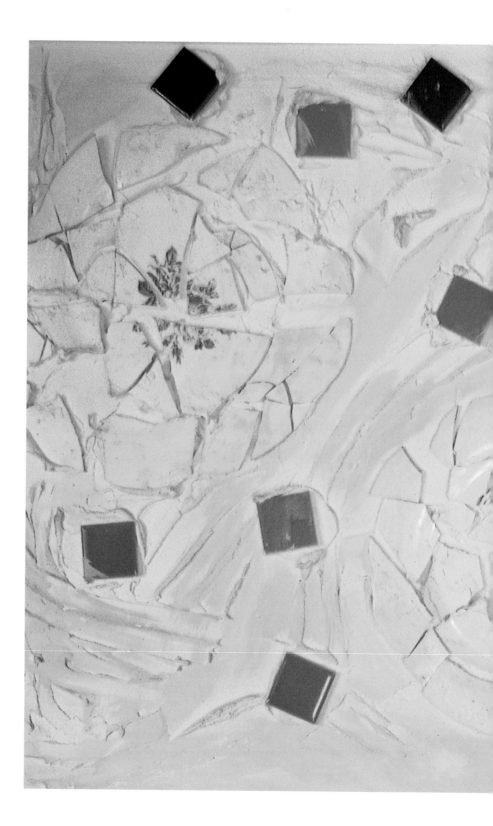

A detail of Geraldine's kitchen mosaic displays her innovative approach to recycling castoff items into a work of art.

make and
believe
realizing our beliefs, goals, and dreams

What most people don't realize is that it's the belief that we find beautiful in the cathedral, or in the "personal temple" of Geraldine Lloyd, the artist and cancer survivor. It is the belief that organizes the artist's vision and makes the work of art.

Opposite: With imagination and humor, Cathi Horton put conventions aside and handcrafted a mosaic fireplace mantel and then turned it into a working fountain for her bedroom. The walls are a pale aqua like the ocean. "After all, I am a water sign. I like the sound of water; it helps me to meditate," she said. The mantel fountain brings a spiritual focal point to the room.

Above: A magic lantern for making wishes was created by Horton from a garage-sale coffee pot. "I just write my wishes on paper and drop them inside," she says.

However, I was not an artistic child prodigy. In fact, I did rather poorly in the one or two art classes I took. Because I had no artistic training, my first acts of belief-based decorating were small do-it-yourself projects: applying a paint-kit glaze to my cabinets, arranging some flowers, or organizing a tabletop photo grouping. It wasn't until I was ensconced in my first home that I discovered my knack for creating beauty in living spaces in the same way many women do. This experience emboldened me and helped me to believe in my own creative power. I began to see the cycle of belief and creativity: The more I created, the more I believed, and the more I believed, the more I created. The cycle continually grew—but it all began with belief.

I began to look for more meaning in life in all that I did. The process led me deeper. I could no longer settle for prepackaged decorating ideas and assembly-line furniture in coordinated sets of the current style. I could no longer tolerate a finished room. Something seemed dead about a room that had no space left for new growth and new artistic expression. The interior spirit of my home began to reflect the state of my own spirit. As long as I was actively creating—bringing positive ideas into view within my home and my life—I had a sense of spiritual health. At last I felt alive inside! As we observed earlier in the examples of church artistry, through creative expression, we have an opportunity to commune with our own Creator— we allow that spirit within us freedom to express itself. To be creative is to be spiritual. There is no great mystery at work here, no special power or gift. The ability is present and available to all of us right now.

When I began to meditate upon my life interests, goals, and dreams, I found I had plenty of ideas to express artistically within my home. I used these as subject matter for my decorating. I soon realized that my power to be creative was only limited by my own life vision—the breadth of my understanding of my own beliefs, values, goals, and dreams. That is where the book of belief came in. I needed to take stock of all that was important to me. I knew that once having identified these spiritual ideals and organized them into a source book, I could use them as inspiration. I started with lists and questions and then found images to represent the concepts I decided were important.

Here are some of the ideas from my own personal book of belief:

With childlike freedom, Cathi created a retro recreation room inspired by pajama parties, bowling alleys, and 1950s television shows. "I only have the things I love and love the things I have," she said. Cathi's objects of affection include vintage furniture and lamps, a 45-rpm record collection and player, a leopard-print rug and pillows, and, of course, her best friend, Scooby the tomcat.

beliefs

1. On the opening page of my book is a copy of Nelson Mandela's inaugural speech in which he says, "As we let our light shine, we give others permission to do the same."

2. A picture of William Morris and a small bit of his handmade wallpaper demonstrates that when we use our hands to make our home's decorations, we get to know the nature of the Creator a little more because we are the unique handmade creations of the Creator.

3. Affirmative letters from an elderly friend encourage me to believe in myself.

values and interests

1. A photo of a moss-covered log in a friend's garden represents a respect for nature and a love of that exact color of moss green.

2. When my grandmother was small, she was very poor and ashamed that she had no fine clothing to wear. In her later life, she and my grandfather became successful, and she loved to buy beautiful suits. My love and respect for my grandparents and the value of their example of fortitude in life are represented in vintage buttons that I keep from my grandmother's clothing.

goals and dreams

1. A small replica of a stained-glass window reminds me that I want to learn to become proficient at making stained-glass windows and other items.

2. A postcard of the Eiffel Tower represents my desire to become fluent in French.

3. A picture of Luciano Pavarotti represents my dream to hear the Three Tenors in concert.

4. A photograph of civil rights heroine Rosa Parks being fingerprinted after refusing to relinquish to racially demeaning laws during the 1960s expresses my dream to see all people treated equally.

These are just a few examples from my ever-growing book of belief.

At first, because I was not a trained professional artist nor accustomed to making things that represented my ideals, I was not quite sure what approach to take next. Inspiration came quite by accident during a visit to a friend's house.

Above: Among Adair Moran's sacred objects is a scarf blessed by the Dalai Lama.

Opposite: Method acting: By surrounding herself with objects and images associated with the theater, Adair can more easily visualize becoming a Broadway actress.

method acting

In Adair Moran's personal space, every wall is a different bold color, like fabrics torn from a harlequin's suit—yellow with turquoise, and purple with black. One big mirrored wall, when looked at from a certain angle, makes all of the other walls overlap in shards of footlight color. Overhead hang wobbly little 1940s-style stage lights

surrounded by day-glo stars affixed to the ceiling in a playful send-up of the starlight ceilings of vintage movie houses. Spaced out on the walls and staircase to Adair's attic room are theater showbills and production posters tacked here and there, resembling the backstage alley of Paris's Moulin Rouge.

The broad wood floor seems fit for a dance rehearsal, with plenty of room for actions and gestures. In this space the presence of the stage is inescapable. Here Adair can visualize herself as an opera diva, chorus dancer, or 1950s movie starlet. She is an aspiring actress, and she keeps her goals clearly in sight. Broadway-bound, here in her room, she's not likely to forget it. Adair was only nine years old when she began this process of bringing her dreams into view within her home. At

this tender age she realized the importance of visualization. Now, at the age of sixteen, she is an expert at belief-based decorating. She said,

When I was twelve, I covered the entire ceiling of my room with posters of actors and actresses I wanted to be like. Everything I do now—including decorating my space—makes me feel like an actor. I live immersed in it. My days are spent in dance lessons, acting class, rehearsals, and performances.

Entering Adair's room was tantamount to walking into a three-dimensional book of belief. She had taken her goals and dreams and created her own stage setting for life. In her room, she actually lives inside the dream. Every moment, from the time she opens her eyes in the morning until she closes them at night, she is reminded of the vision she holds dear. For her, the childhood concept of make-believe has become a very effective process of dream fulfillment. She paints walls in theatrical colors, hangs mirrors in which to view her dance rehearsals, displays Broadway posters, and even fabricates costumes. Then she believes in her ability to accomplish the goal of becoming a Broadway actress, which in her space isn't hard to do.

Adair's mother, Victoria, joined her daughter in a communal belief-based decorating project—painting the bedroom area of the attic apartment. By helping Adair in this endeavor, she gave her daughter an affirmative vote of belief in the young actress's ability to fulfill her ambitions.

It seems Adair's method is working, too. Chosen through a grueling audition process, she has spent two summers in New York City at the American Academy of Dramatic Arts. She played the lead role of Eva Schlessinger in the stage play *Kindertransport,* the story of a young girl's escape from Nazi Germany.

Through the action of belief-based decorating, Adair has given form to a longing of her spirit. And as she experiences the atmosphere daily, her ability to believe in the completion of her goal is increased.

a spiritual reality

When we were small, it was so easy to believe. We need only to observe a small child or young person like Adair to reacquaint ourselves with this truth.

Opposite: A stagelike room, complete with mirror and ballet barre, help this young actress to live inside of her dream. A favorite show tune and other musical influences make the atmosphere of rehearsal complete. A personalized director's chair makes the fantasy seem real.

Right: Cathi Horton transformed a vintage refrigerator into a television cabinet. Decoupaged to the door is her favorite—Marilyn Monroe.

We are all born believing. For a time when we are small, we believe no one will ever hurt us, we are deserving of unconditional love, life is an interesting adventure, and Mom and Dad are the most heroic people in the universe. Most of us never question it. We are born with these ideas and accept them as truth.

In addition, as children we easily accept fantasy stories such as *Alice in Wonderland*. While children might acknowledge the unlikelihood of a

talking rabbit leading them on a madcap journey down a long tunnel, it doesn't seem to matter at all. Children usually know that a rabbit can't talk or that a special potion can't make them small; however, they harbor a secret hope that someday something unexpected—something magical and mystical—just might happen! This is what I call a

spiritual reality. The unseen is just as real as the seen. We believe in the hidden potential of our spirit to manifest something special in our lives, and fairy tales and fantasies feed this hope.

"Let's pretend . . ." These were the favorite words of Alice Liddell, the little girl who inspired Lewis Carroll to write *Alice in Wonderland*. After he

had spontaneously created the story on an afternoon picnic with Alice, she begged him to make a book of the tale. In 1865 the Victorian story that

Above: Using a waxy iron-on transfer, paper roses and photographs were applied to fabric. Heat-transfer paper can be purchased at most art or craft centers; results may vary so experiment first.

was to become known as one of the most imaginative children's stories of all time was finally published. But, having taken several years to get into print, Carroll lamented that Alice was probably too old to even care about it:

> *It's a pity that girls have to grow up. They're a lot more fun when they are small; they love stories and other good things. When they turn into elegant ladies, they become very boring.*

Even little Alice, who loved to "pretend" a fantasy was a reality, succumbed to Dodgson's worst fear: she outgrew her imagination. She eventually went on to sell the priceless handwritten manuscript of the story at a public auction.

Children naturally seem to know what they need. Like magpie nests, their rooms are typically a collection of favorite things—baubles, souvenirs, pictures of their heroes: scientists, super heroes, athletes, musicians, and movie stars. They collect stamps, dolls, rocket ships, planetary models, horse statues, records, and books. Ant farms and musical instruments sit side by side, challenging even the most talented of parents to new feats of storage wizardry. Drawings are taped to the walls, handmade beaded necklaces (in progress) loop the lamp on the nightstand, and paints (often left open), along with crayons strewn about, give the impression of a life-giving creative explosion, not merely a mess that needs cleaning up. Children are far more concerned with what they can make than with being neat. They reside in a spirit-filled place of curiosity and joyous expression.

In an unusually mature decision to pursue a specific dream, our aspiring actress Adair turned her room into an example of a conscious use of belief-based decorating to help her achieve her goal. She has taken the concept of visualization, or attempting to lucidly imagine herself as an actress, to another level of reality. By actually living on a stage, she lives out her goal. In the stage setting for the life she has created, she is actually playing the part and is already living as if the dream were a reality.

At first glance it may seem a stretch to say that the atmosphere Adair has created bears any similarity to the approach of medieval church artisans, but it is rooted in the same premise because Adair has physical evidence of her creativity.

Really, it shouldn't be surprising that we find so much belief and creativity in the bedroom of such a young person. Many religious traditions around the world include stories extolling the virtues of childlike faith. The Bible teaches us "to have the faith of a child" and "it is done unto us as we believe."

In the works of writer C. S. Lewis, we find tales of childhood make-believe that many scholars say actually parallel concepts that are found in Christianity. In his series of children's books *The Chronicles of Narnia*, it is belief, or childlike faith, that is the key to entering the noble land of Narnia. In these stories, once a child reaches a certain age, he or she can no longer visit Narnia, which is a place of talking animals and mythical creatures such as centaurs and fauns. Many of the characters are imbued with idyllic chivalry and honor.

In one Narnia story, the children and their friend Puddleglum, a poignantly funny little creature who constantly struggles with negative

Opposite: Cathi hand painted a cotton comforter with words and patterns borrowed from vintage fabrics. Pillow shams were made to match. Note the vintage dial phone and organza gown sitting atop the bedspread.

Let's connect the ideas of Adair and Cathi to some exercises that will help you to further your own belief-based decorating process. If you are still feeling a little fear about your own abilities, relax. *The artist is not a special kind of person, but each person is a special kind of artist.* You will find your own special kind of creativity.

Let's pretend we are going on an archaeological field trip to dig up bits and pieces of a forgotten past—our past. If you can, go back to the house and bedroom of your youth, even if the bedroom has been redecorated. (If going there is not literally possible, take the trip in your imagination.) Think of the activities you did there. What were your hobbies and interests? How did you represent these in your room?

Use words to paint as clear a picture as you can of your childhood bedroom. You may have to pick a certain period of your youth, because children often change their interests several times. What were your dreams? How did you express them in your room? What kinds of creative supplies did you keep handy? Children's rooms are always loaded with inspiration and tools: markers, clay, stamps, drawing pencils, books, and others. Describe your childhood room in as much detail as possible. Reconnect yourself with that world of spiritual reality.

If you have been able to revisit your childhood home, proceed on to the attic, garage, or basement—the places where you might find remnants of your childhood. Ask your parents about the old photo albums. A good researcher is thorough and appreciates hard evidence. Here are some possibilities:

artworks or things you made—from drawings to potholders

art materials—crayons, chalk, kits

awards—trophies, medals, or citations

books—your favorites

collections—stamps, seashells, dolls

clubs—What were you involved in at school?

family—gifts, keepsakes, heirlooms

inspiring words—notes from teachers, parents, or friends

interests—Did you love new clothing? Dancing? Going to the movies?

music—What records did you own? Did you play an instrument or sing?

personal heroes or icons—people you admired

photos—look for "candid" shots: pictures of you being funny or uninhibited, wearing a costume or making a crazy face

science projects—microscopes, model rockets, or electronics sets

sports—your old basketball, ice skates, or baseball glove

List all your data, including what each of these archaeological finds might have meant to the young heart and mind that owned them. Look for the symbolism. For example: a picture of John F. Kennedy can represent hope, youthful vision, and service to mankind. Why did you identify with this man? Does he still inspire you? Are you reminded of a forgotten value?

In all this digging around (physically and mentally) you may find a few objects or images that are not empowering symbols for you. Spend time with the feeling and let this experience help you understand how material images and objects can compel our spirits in both positive and negative ways. That is what you are after here: to become aware of the empowering effect the right images can have upon you spiritually. When you know this, you can intentionally make your environment visually uplifting in the same way you did as a child.

the question "why?"

Using the same list as in the previous exercise, look around your home for evidence of your current interests, goals, and dreams. Here is a sample questionnaire designed to help you recognize them. By asking the question "Why?" of yourself—in the same way children constantly do—you can take the quality of your answers and understanding to a new level. You will be able to establish the spiritual reality or dream that the interest represents for you.

- What periods in history attract you? Why?
- Who do you admire? Why?
- What books and authors are your favorites? Why?
- What kinds of art do you like and who are your favorite artists? Why?
- What places in the world do you love most? Where would you like to visit? Why?
- What are your favorite plays and movies? Why?
- What are your personal areas of interest? Why?
- What is your favorite quote or saying? Why?
- What are your favorite colors? How do they make you feel? Why?

book of belief update

In the last chapter, we focused on defining beliefs and values and then representing them in your book of belief. Now take this opportunity to expand your inspirations to include your interests, goals, and dreams. Allow the answers you have just arrived at to indicate images that can be used in your book. For example: fix little paint-store samples of your favorite colors to a page; be sure to describe why you like them. Or find a picture of a dream destination.

Get creative! Remember, you can draw, computer-generate symbols and quotes, use photos, clip magazines or newspapers, or just write about it; you are limited only by your imagination—and it is limitless!

make a dream box

What is a dream box? A shoe-box-sized model room that focuses on your goals and dreams. So this is your first opportunity to play with these new concepts. Take a current dream or one from your childhood and create a little room about it. Remember playing paper dolls or dress-up? This project is a little of both with a bit of method acting as well. Think of Adair's space. She has posters of actors she admires, costume pieces hung on the walls, theater-like colors and lighting,

plenty of room to practice choreography, and a mirror and ballet barre. Her environment supports her dream. She has combined various elements from the world of theater to evoke a feeling of being immersed in the dream.

Target any idea you are working on fulfilling—perhaps owning a business, learning to make pottery, becoming a writer, or attracting a love partner. Make a list of all the positive aspects or benefits of your dream. When it has come true, what does it look like? You say you would like to become a writer, so what will your desk look like? Where will you live—downtown Manhattan or a chateau in the French countryside? What is the view from your desk? What writers do you admire and pattern yourself after? What will you wear? Are the walls painted or papered and in what color? Are there windows? Who do you envision in the room with you? What tools of the trade will there be—a computer or just pen and paper?

In a recent Habitat for Humanity workshop I was teaching, a vivacious woman named Gloria decided to create her model room around her dream of owning a soul-food restaurant. She envisioned a charming little 1950s-style diner where she'd serve her Kansas City barbecued ribs, potato salad, and baked beans. For dessert, she would bring out a scratch cake topped with a foothill of buttercream icing.

The red, white, and chrome interior of the restaurant would look out onto a southern front porch. A sign suspended above the parking lot, which she sees filled with vintage Cadillacs, Chevrolets, and Ford pickup trucks, would announce "Gloria's Place" in neon. And, back inside, Nat King Cole would croon a love song on the jukebox. How, you may wonder, did Glo fit all that into a shoe box? Here is how she managed.

In typical style, Glo modified the project to suit herself—she used a grocery box instead. Taking the opportunity to really get into the spirit of childhood, she started by playing house—or diner; tiny cakes and cookies were made to fit onto the tabletop she had created. The tables and chairs were made by folding cardboard notebook backs thinking, are trapped in the underworld with the evil witch who tries to sabotage their belief in the beautiful Narnian world and good King Aslan. But finally, Puddleglum masters his thoughts and declares,

> *Suppose we have only dreamed, or made up, all those things—trees and grass and sun and moon and stars and Aslan himself. Suppose we have. Then all I can say is that the made-up things seem a good deal more important than the real ones. . . . That is why I am going to stand by the play-world. I'm on Aslan's side even if there isn't any Aslan to lead it. I'm going to live like a Narnian . . . even if there isn't any Narnia.*

These allegories of Lewis's suggest the possibility of creating our own reality by directing our thoughts through belief and actions. Although he has been called a writer for children, in these cynical times he should be considered a writer for adults, too.

Lucy, I'm home

Few among us can truthfully say we have the freedom to just be ourselves—uninhibitedly expressing joy as we did when we were children. Once in a great while, though, we meet someone who greets every day—every experience—with the abandon of a child on summer vacation. One such person is Cathi Horton.

One day, just for fun, Cathi grabbed a black crayon and decided the walls of the all-white kitchen would look better wearing nickel-sized polka dots. She worked furiously turning the basic little kitchen into her own playroom. Cathi isn't nine like Adair; she's thirty-nine, but her sense of childlike fun and adventure is still with her. Not only does Cathi decorate her walls with crayons, she also hangs curtains on the outside of her house and uses paper dolls of Hollywood movie stars to decorate her Christmas tree. She keeps a bag of wigs for dressing up and a magic lantern for making wishes. It is a magical little house of make and . . . believe.

Cathi believes it is important to have fun and satisfy her playful and creative urges. "For years I tried to be like everyone else and take a conservative approach to life," she says, "but I became very depressed trying to deny my creative urges and funny nature. Finally, I decided it was them or me." She's no longer concerned about the resale value of her house or what her parents, friends, or neighbors will think. She says "I love bright—you might say electric—colors so I just painted my living-room walls in chartreuse and turquoise diamonds. Also, I converted a vintage refrigerator into a TV cabinet—complete with a life-sized Marilyn Monroe applied to the front. I hung some 1950s curtains in the eating area close by my leopard-print diner booth. I am carrying the vintage idea all through the house because I just love Hollywood during that period, especially the old sitcoms like *I Love Lucy*. Times were more glamorous then. For my bedroom, I created a chair with pictures of movie-star couples on it . . . helps me to visualize love in my life. Now, if only I had a good-looking Latin man so I could yell, 'Oohh, Rickyyyyy!'"

Cathi has learned to value her unique creative spirit and the expressions of that spirit more than the opinion of anyone else. She has reconnected with her own childlike sense of creativity, and this loyalty to her fun-loving nature is paying off. Since Cathi has begun to take a more lighthearted approach to her home and surrounded herself with her own artistry that expresses her ideas, she has developed some even bigger dreams. She is now writing and producing stage shows and is involved in a pilot for a television show that will demonstrate to viewers how they can bring more fun into their lives.

masterpiece anxiety

Children will try anything. They run, jump, and finger paint, all with the same abandon. It is this kind of exuberance, or joy in the process, that characterizes Cathi's approach to life—and decorating. She has interwoven the two in a way that makes her home a constantly evolving canvas for her spirit. Like a child's naive rendering of a little cottage with the sun smiling brightly overhead, Cathi's house is her own image of a fun-filled and joyful life. She simply responds to what she loves and then "paints" it into her space. Spontaneous in array, like a child's room, it doesn't always coordinate in the fashion of the styled-to-perfection interiors of glossy design magazines. Rather, it conveys the real-life vitality of a painterly collage.

The pressure many of us feel when we contemplate decorating our homes can be paralyzing. As adults, we view most of our endeavors as a final proving ground; unless we see immediate results, we assume we have no talent. We become so product-focused that we fail to enjoy the process. For Cathi and Adair, art and decorating projects are mostly about the process of self-expression. Both of them have kept touch with, or rediscovered, their youthful exuberance, and it is evident not only in their surroundings, but in the way they live their lives. By creating areas and making and collecting objects that represent their interests, children and adults intuitively are performing their own versions of the ritual of belief, demonstrating that spontaneity can be revitalized at any age.

and stapling them together; then a chrome finish was suggested by spraying them with silver paint. On the wall, a computer-generated menu listed her fare; hamhocks and greens, sweet-potato pie, and more. Miniature curtains in a red-and-white check were hot-glued into place at the windows. And just outside you could see her neon sign.

dream box to dream room

Begin to envision a space in your home in which a real-life version of your Dream Box can be created. It needn't be a whole room; a wall area or corner will do. The idea is to get your dreams in front of you and bring them into real-life format. Remember, seeing is believing. Start by simply displaying the images from your box: posters, photos, statues, books, and articles that relate to your dream.

the *creative*
greenhouse

we are all artists by nature

Little children blow around Claudia's skirt like fallen leaves; others cling to her branches. She is a dryad, or tree spirit, and even more. Her skin is the color of rich soil, and fields of cotton swathe her ample body.

Opposite: Earthy colors, textures, and materials remind Claudia Cooper of nature's creativity. She says that nature inspires her inherent creativity.

Above: A found branch, embellished with rope, becomes a curtain rod for a valance of tribal fabric.

Rock formations of aquamarine dangle from silver lightning at her ears. Prehistoric amber encircles her wrist. This earth mother, Claudia, is tree and soil, mountain and bird. Her songs lilt forth like celestial narration; her simple guitar, a harp for our time.

At home in her light-filled apartment, she looks like an outcropping of her fertile green walls. In fact, every wall in her space is the same shade of leaf green. And, it is as easy to inhabit as a forest glade. The seasoned oak floor is bare underfoot, and recycled benches and tables form a ring of conversation. A stained-glass lantern of family lineage is poised for illumination, and tribal musical instruments made from exotic materials hang on the walls. There are Kenyan cloth and a loom for weaving. Dried flowers and vines add to the creative compost. In this, her spiritual greenhouse, Claudia is cultivating her own organic creativity.

Claudia has used the natural world as inspiration for her house of belief. What she has created is actually a life-sized dream box. Claudia's dream is simply to live creatively, which for her means to live naturally, because the concepts found in nature reassure her of her own creativity. She describes it this way:

Just look around you to see that creativity is the spirit of nature—and of God. Everything is growing. If we would just leave our natural world alone, it would continue on in balance and harmony. I have realized that I must acknowledge my own creativity. To assure myself that I am indeed creative, I must make my home as much like the natural world as possible so that I spontaneously make things and create without becoming too self-conscious about it. I had some experiences when I was growing up that challenged my ability to believe that I am creative. So now I go to great lengths to make an environment that makes me know that I am creative and that it is good to express myself in this way.

Claudia has written her own prescription for that which once ailed her spirit—demeaning childhood memories. Before she could write a prescription, she had to get to the root of her problem. She shared with me the root of the weed that had tangled her garden.

When I was about five years old, I had expressed a love of music. Everyone who knew me at my church said I had great potential. So, when my family moved into a house with a piano in the sunroom, I went straight for the keyboard. This was my chance to learn to play. However, my mother sold the piano—she said we didn't have room for it. I was brokenhearted. Also, we had moved into a mostly white subdivision, and we were one of the few black families in the neighborhood. In the '60s, there was a lot of racism, as you know, and we were treated badly. The piano could have

helped me to have a goal and a dream in the midst of those difficulties. From then on I had a hard time thinking of my creativity as having value, because my mother hadn't valued it then. Later, when I was in high school, my family did buy a piano—and my mother put it in the sunroom.

artistic license

Many of those I have worked with over the years and with whom I have shared my philosophy of belief-based decorating are very much like Claudia—and me. At first they find it hard to believe that they are naturally creative and that creativity has value. And it really is no wonder that they have these perceptions. Today, most of us think of the artist as someone who exhibits in galleries or sings in concert halls. We have bought into the idea that there are only a gifted few who can consort with the muses. Even though the artist appears privileged, many would point out the volatile aspects of the creative lifestyle, recalling the tortured-artist syndrome.

The classic example of the tortured-artist syndrome is that of Vincent van Gogh. "The more I am spent, ill, a broken pitcher," he wrote, "by so much more I am an artist—a creative artist."

Indeed, testimony like this would lead us to believe that the artistic life is anything but positive—or healthy. Taking the self-conscious ego-driven approach to art can be a downward spiral

Claudia's living room is just that—a room devoted to living pursuits. It includes plants for tending, books for reading, musical instruments for playing, a loom for weaving, and seating for conversation with friends. A colorful array of the sofa and pillows' mixed ethnic prints, along with the light streaming in from the windows and open door, make this an inviting place to sit and visit. A vivid yellow vase atop the rustic coffee table becomes the focal point of the room.

with a destination of substance addiction, mental illness, obsession, and, finally, sad death. Our century has seen its share of casualties in every creative medium: musicians—Jim Morrison and Janis Joplin; painters—Jackson Pollock and Mark Rothko; poets—Sylvia Plath and Jack Kerouac; and actors—James Dean and Judy Garland, to list only a few. In his nineteenth-century essay "Art," Ralph Waldo Emerson wrote: "Thus is art vilified; the name conveys to the mind its secondary and bad senses; it stands in the imagination as somewhat contrary to nature, and struck with death from the first."

Emerson concurs that spiritual estrangement seems to be the modern requirement for artists. In fact, we worship these destructive models as heroes or martyrs—those touched with the gilded paintbrush. We say that these celebrated artists are "gifted." Product-oriented art is their domain. With works of art for sale, their private struggles become marketing fodder for commerce-driven art dealers who shrewdly formulate for them a romantic mystique. This kind of capitalistic approach to art has become full blown in the twentieth century, introducing the idea that there are two distinct groups among us—those who are artists and those who aren't. This elitist mind-set has served only to push us farther from our inherent creativity to express ourselves artistically. What is implicit with the tortured-artist model is that creativity must come from experiences of lack—a lost love, economic poverty, or mental illness. When, in truth, creativity is limitless and constantly available as well as normal and healthy; the more

Claudia's heirloom lamp is complemented by rocks, shells, seeds, and conifers found on nature walks. Growing nearby in jars and boxes are herbs and cuttings for drying and wreath-making. An ethnic-print textile serves as a striking tapestry on the wall. Contrasted against the textile is a white cutout metal chair.

Claudia expressed her creativity, the more she was returned to a sense of mental and spiritual well-being. We need only to look at nature to see it illustrated clearly.

the living room

During Emerson's time (1803–82), creativity came as naturally as breathing. The Victorians saw no distinction between the creative energy that flowed through nature—ever expanding, changing, and diversifying, from seed to flower to compost and back again. Artistic ideas were as expected by them as sunrise or nightfall. In fact, at the height of Morris's Arts and Crafts movement, many a parlor took on the appearance of a summer garden grown out of control.

Wallpapers and fabrics were printed with leaves, blooms, trees, and birds—any motif found on a walk through the woods. Cuttings were dried and pressed for wall hangings or souvenir books. Recently, at my favorite rare-book store, I came across a small Victorian traveling book. The little wood-covered document was actually a combined dried-flower press and journal, with travel recorded by the natural findings of each day. Under each verdant entry could be found a handwritten description: where the sample was found, other events that occurred that day, and a comparison of the mounted leaf or bloom to an aspect of the trip. One entry from a page with a silver maple leaf read:

The light here in Notting shimmers like the leaves from this maple. All is moving, rather transient. I am restless. Have as many ideas as profuse foliage from this tree. Preparing for harvest, I look homeward.

This nineteenth-century writer chose to represent the days of his travels with natural

images. He even goes so far as to say his thoughts are as prolific as leaves on a tree—and as naturally occurring. In this case, direct contact with nature inspired the writer to poetic phrasing and stimulated his thinking as he alluded to a feeling of creative abundance: "Have as many ideas as profuse foliage. . . ."

Here, the author uses symbolism, comparing his ideas to leaves and the anticipation of creative expression as "preparing for harvest." This ability to describe one object in terms of another—to think symbolically—is basic to most forms of artistic expression. It's a skill that we have begun to cultivate in our own books of belief, by finding images that symbolically represent our beliefs, values, goals, and dreams. Its daily practical use allowed Victorians to stay connected to their creative spirits, helping them to identify the underlying similarities in all of creation. Here we can see how artistic thinking and spiritual thinking become nearly one and the same; both are concerned with representing transcendent themes through the use of symbols.

Consider a Victorian hair weaving. Those who have seen one of these handcrafts are not likely to have forgotten it. Often a braid of hair from a deceased loved one was crafted into a commemorative wall hanging, sculpted into an animal shape or nature scene, or simply embellished with flowers or beads. To us this practice may seem macabre, but to the Victorians it was a very natural activity. The hair—like fallen leaves—enshrined and braided together concepts of life, death, and the cycle of creative energy.

By today's standards, nineteenth-century life was a work of art. Although very few people during that time would have considered themselves artists in the same way few people today proclaim that title, nearly everyone expressed his or her own kind of artistry. By allowing the natural creativity that was observed in nature to empower it, Victorian life was an artistic expression.

Creative abundance: A table setting for one of Claudia's renowned dinners includes her handmade gemstone napkin rings, hand-dipped candles, hand-painted table, and homegrown flowers, arranged in an interesting grouping of recycled cobalt bottles. In fact, very little in her light-filled apartment does not reflect her natural creativity. Claudia's home is uniquely her own.

Embracing the Victorian concept that we are all naturally creative is an important step in belief-based decorating, because we can only create a house of belief by bringing our positive ideas into physical form through creative actions. We must have a sense of self-confidence that there is something within us to express and that we have the faculties to do it. Even if we have never called ourselves creative, we may have considered ourselves resourceful or clever or industrious. Somehow it is easier to use these words, which are really synonyms for creative, than it is to actually use the "C" word. We typically use these alternative terms for those in creative work outside the arts.

We casually use our ingenuity everyday. One day Ruth, a client who didn't consider herself to be creative, told me about her day at work as a pediatric nurse:

We have a little boy in intensive care who suffered burns in a fireworks accident. He is in a lot of pain and refused to allow us to change his bandages. The one thing that seems to help him make it through the day is when his mother reads to him. He likes history and science. In fact, his mother said he had been working on a science-fair project at home. It has to do with the rain forest and the medicines found in the leaves and plants there. So, I asked him to pretend he had been wounded in the rain forest and that we were going to apply a primitive medicine from a flower we found there. And he let us change the dressing!

Ruth's solution is as creative a concept as we have ever heard. But, because of the limiting definition of artist or designer in our modern world, she hadn't considered herself part of the creative contingent.

Ruth is indeed creative—and she was even willing to admit it after I pointed out that she had

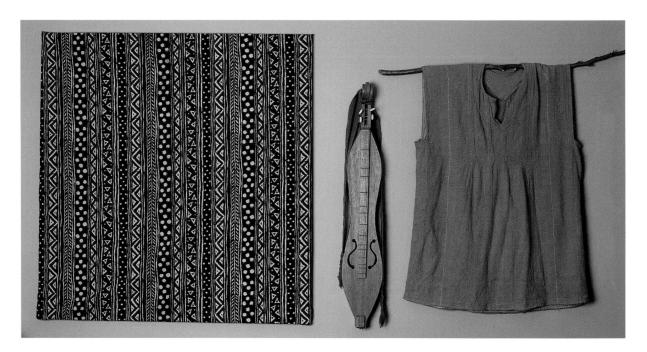

written the plot line of a story set in the rain forest to help in persuading the boy. "Creative maybe, but an artist—that is a person who can make you see, or think, or hear something in a unique or higher way—I'm no artist."

Ruth's definition of an artist is one I think we can all live with. It has nothing to do with gallery shows or recording contracts. She suggests that artists express and help us to recognize meaning. We may find it artistic when truth or beauty is represented in a way that speaks to our heart. Literature, paintings, and music are where we commonly look for artistic transcendence because waiting in rush-hour traffic or cleaning the kitchen leaves us feeling anything but artistic or spiritual. But once we start to be aware of it, to look for it, real-life artistry is taking place all around us.

To find meaning, we must be looking for it. When we enter a museum and stroll around a sculpture, we are expecting to find something—an insight, a revelation, something exquisite. When we go to a church or temple we expect to be touched within our spirits. But when we get in the car and go to the grocery store, play with the children, or just do our jobs as Ruth did, we find we aren't looking for epiphanies and eternal truths to spring up. We don't expect to find art in everyday experiences; but the truth is that art is an everyday experience when we begin to expect it.

Claudia's world

In Claudia's house of belief, all of the rooms are *living* rooms where she grows new ideas and artistic expression. Anytime of day or night I find her in the midst of some new project—from candle making to sewing her own clothing. In every room

A collection of African textiles, instruments, and clothing pay tribute to Claudia's ethnicity. Her heritage is a rich source of inspiration for her and her visitors and another example of her prolific creativity.

in her home there is at least one area devoted to a living pursuit: a desk for making hand-stamped stationary in her studio, a weaving loom in the front room, musical instruments for open-air concerts near the porch, and plenty of handmade table settings in the dining area for her famous dinner parties.

The only difference between people like Claudia and Ruth is that one is actively working to resolve her doubts about the value of her creativity, thereby opening herself to the opportunity for artistic perceptions in everyday life, and the other is not. Even though Claudia has struggled to accept her own creativity, she has written her own prescription for what ailed her creative spirit—demeaning childhood memories. She is resolving her negative perceptions within her home. She uses the ritual of belief as a proactive method of creative acceptance.

In some ways, Claudia is like the children at the Montessori school where she now teaches: she seems to just know what she needs to keep her creativity and her spirit alive. As we discussed earlier, children's rooms provide the right greenhouse elements for their natural creativity to thrive. In a more adult way Claudia has done the same. She uses nature as a symbol of prolific creativity, then she models her home after it. She has gathered art materials and inspiration around her like sun and rain around the earth. The resulting atmosphere—like pure oxygen breathed in—is one of meaning.

In Claudia's world everything is intentional; even the most functional of elements signify an idea. In the case of her recycled furniture, it is a respect for the environment and a disdain for rampant consumerism. She says:

The source of my furniture isn't as important as the very essence of the piece; it could be someone's

a walk in the woods

Take the first opportunity you can to get back to nature. Anything from a week-long hiking trip to a walk through Central Park will do. Observe the plant life; let yourself be inspired by its diversity and profusion. Study a tree; notice the sheer abundance of its leaves. Sit on the grass and look deep into the blades at a world within the world. Note the little insects, spiders, worms, and animals. Under a canopy of trees notice the forest floor—the natural compost. If you like the Victorian plant-journal idea, begin yours or just gather fallen leaves, rocks, shells, branches, and blooms along the way as take-home reminders of the creative abundance you have observed.

Nature's ornaments can be incorporated into a belief-based home in many ways. Here are just a few ideas:

♦ Tree branches make interesting curtain rods.

♦ Fallen leaves can be used as stencil patterns for the walls or floor.

♦ Pinecones can make finials—the finishing ornaments at the ends of your curtain rods or the corners of your bed frame.

♦ Seashells can be added to a mosaic pot or wall, or fixed right to the wall as a decorative border.

♦ Rocks can be collected for the bowl of a fountain.

♦ Flowers can be dried for wreaths and table settings.

♦ Nature's color palette can be used to create a nurturing and comfortable setting; remember, Claudia painted every wall in her home leaf green, and her natural creativity is thriving.

If you would like to create permanent affirmations of nature's creativity, you can imprint fabrics with images of the blooms, leaves, and shells you have collected by using the heat of the sun.

the atmospheric elements

Sun, seeds, soil, and water are just a few of the requirements for organic creativity. These contribute to our earthly atmosphere of creative abundance. Like the balanced greenhouse atmosphere of the earth, our homes need to have the right atmospheric elements, too, for artistic activity to germinate. An art-studio environment can be just a well-equipped greenhouse. Raw materials make spontaneous creativity possible. Now is the time to gather your artistic elements together.

Begin by taking a field trip to your nearest art or hobby store. Don't be afraid to ask questions of the staff. They are usually art students themselves and very happy to share information with you. I have formulated a starter list for you; these are just a few of the essentials you will need for some of the activities in the coming chapters. Please don't allow a moment of intimidation to enter your head or heart here; belief-based home decorating is a more meaningful and artistic approach. It is also accessible to anyone. It is, in fact, the gentlest introduction to artistry imaginable. Over the next few chapters we will be simply doodling. Just relax and have fun.

The following items will be used in the next few chapters:

- 1 set of 24 watercolor markers, medium to fine-tip
- 1 set of 12 colored pencils
- 1 scale ruler
- 1 tablet of 1/4-inch-scale grid paper
- 1 (8 x 12-inch) drawing tablet
- 1 HB hard pencil
- 1 gum eraser
- Miscellaneous: scissors, glue stick, White Out, and tape

castoffs or an antique-store find. I find the greatest raw materials for my home by simply driving down the street. That chest over there was a curbside find, and those chairs I found in a trash dumpster. I like to transform things. Working with castoffs frees me creatively; I am not afraid to try something different.

She also offers three good tips for those who struggle with masterpiece anxiety:

First: Use what you have—from recycled empty cans to family furniture hand-me-downs.

Second: Remember that mistakes can be opportunities. There have been many times when I have tried a new technique and bungled it, and then created something new and unique from what was at first a mistake. It forces you into really creative thinking to salvage it.

Third: There is more than one way to do anything. Often, I start with one technique and end up doing it a whole different way. You must be flexible—and determined.

Claudia brings up an important point: when we are just beginning to express ourselves in an artistic way, we can feel vulnerable—afraid of making mistakes. But when we create the perfect greenhouse atmosphere, we can control the conditions, decide what to grow, and provide all of the right elements to assure maximum creativity—or harvest. In order for us to model nature, taking its creative principles as our own, we should re-touch with it, keeping our goals in mind.

Previous page: Claudia's studio provides all the atmospheric elements for her creativity to thrive.

Above: A creative compost: This ritual of belief uses past hurts, disappointments, and failures as compost for new personal growth.

a creative compost

During your walk in the woods, you may have noticed the forest floor and the natural compost that gathers there, or what is left of something that once lived. This energy form is in the process of changing—becoming part of a new life form. Now, apply the same principle to the past experiences of your own life. Good or bad, the remains of your past life can be used to fertilize your new creative growth.

New hybrid perceptions sprout out of the waste of past hurts, lost loves, and perceived wrong choices. It is at the time of germination that the potential for artistry arises; then we are able to accept the role of our past in the creation of the present and future. For example, Claudia used the pain of her mother's rejection of her piano talent to fuel her current artistic expressions. If we can artistically piece together the seasons of our lives and find the meaning, we are on the verge of making the transformation from simply being creative to that of artist.

a ritual of belief
part one

This ritual of belief is designed to help you bring past experiences together symbolically to fertilize new creative growth in your life. Here are the steps:

1. Fill a clay pot at least eight inches wide with a creative compost.

Recipe for creative compost: Think of past experiences that need a new perspective or to be released. You might want to make a list before you proceed. Now prepare to fill the pot with soil. With each handful (using your hands because you will feel more connected to the process), think of an experience from your past that you would like to release. Allow these thoughts to be compost for the soil.

2. Plant a seed or cutting of your favorite plant in the composted soil. Name the planting. For example, call it "creativity" and then watch it grow.

a human mosaic
part two

You can add a further empowering step to this ritual by embellishing the outside of your clay pot with bits of mosaic tile. This activity will help you to transform the broken pieces of your experience into an artistic creation. This ritual of belief should be done silently as a meditation.

Before you begin, make a list of all the areas of your life you would like to bring together or acknowledge. List all of your very best attributes. This is a good time for admitting the truly good and undeniably creative aspects of who you are. Think back to Ruth, the pediatric nurse who used her creativity on the job to help the boy with burns. List all of the ways that you are creative—at home, with children, on the job, or, more directly, in an art or craft form. Examples: cooking, clothing, computer skills, communication, expressing love to others, painting, writing letters, and others.

_____

_____

_____

_____

_____

_____

_____

_____

_____

_____

Turn over the pieces of the mosaic tiles; on the back, label each piece with one of these attributes; or, using a paint marker, write the idea directly on the front of the tile so that it will serve as a constant visual affirmation of your best features. Now slowly and deliberately put the pieces in place, allowing the pieces of who you are to become an artistic creation before your very eyes.

the *mind's* eye

using artistic intuition

When we begin to think like artists, we start to find meaning in even the most common occurrences. It is this emphasis on meaning and symbolism that distinguishes belief-based decorating from any other approach to interior design.

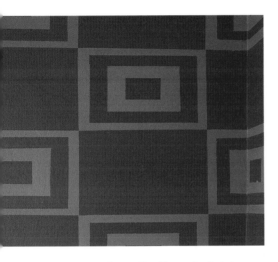

Opposite: The colorful geometry of a favorite painting inspired the tangerine-and-red rectangular-grid pattern in Rod Parks's dining room. A mix of modern furniture—including a George Nelson hanging lamp, Eero Saarinen table, and an Arne Jacobsen famous egg chair—is visually bound together by the strong background.

Above: Artist Bernie Koehrson assisted Rod in bringing out his inner vision to his outer life by measuring, taping, and painting each repeat of the concentric pattern.

Without meaning in home decorating—the expression of our beliefs, values, goals, and dreams—we have only a pointless display of material goods. We might argue that function—a chair to sit on or a shade for the window—has a point to it, and we are right. But as spiritual beings, we are compelled to do so much more. Without our own creative input, our home interiors become no more than a collection of meaningless objects. Life is an artwork of the grandest proportions, and we have been invited to collaborate. We get to paint our own portion of the scene within our homes.

To make a home that not only expresses the soul but delights the eye, we must be able to do more than just think like an artist; we must be able to see like an artist as well. To do so, we must remove ourselves for just a little while from the inner realm of meaning and focus on the purely physical, or outer, world.

the way things look

Beauty is relative; what may look beautiful to one person—a Jackson Pollock splatter painting, for example—may be visual chaos to another. The ordered lines of a neoclassical mansion that a friend finds harmonious may mean architectural nap time for us. The pristinely trimmed and organized topiaries of an eighteenth-century garden may conflict with a penchant for wildflower excess. Yet, the English rose wallpaper in our mother's dining room makes the head spin. It makes no sense at all; how can someone love a wildflower garden—spontaneous and random—and yet despise a wallpaper that conveys the same idea? Things get more puzzling as we notice that although we disdain the predictable rhythm of neoclassical architecture, when we are hanging our favorite Pollock print in a space of utter simplicity and rhythm, the print is more itself than ever. It can be really confusing, even infuriating. Just when we think we have figured out what it is that we like, our eyes contradict us.

This subjective nature of beauty, or visual appeal, explains why the mystique of artistic creativity has endured. Mythology requires an element of intrigue or the unknowable to exist. In the 1880s the mystic artist William Blake expressed that we look through the eyes but do not use the eyes to see. He implies that there is much more to see if we are only looking from within. This notion that we simply use our sight to navigate physically through life has become an utter truth today. Because of the pace of our modern lives and the estrangement of the creative spirit felt by those who work in areas outside the arts, we have stopped using our intuitive sense of beauty and have lost track of how to create from it. The aesthetic eye of which Blake speaks is sleeping.

In his glamorous throwback bedroom sitting area, Rod keeps company with a curvaceous bombshell of a sofa by Vladimir Kagan and a shapely Isamu Noguchi cocktail table. "Seeing someone else get a piece of furniture at a sale or auction that I have fallen in love with is like losing a girlfriend," he says.

In the twentieth century, we move so swiftly that we rarely see what is going on within our own neighborhoods. Most of us have driven down the same street day after day for weeks, months, and even years, and then suddenly notice a feature on a building—an interesting Greek frieze, for example—that has been there all along. And even within our homes we look past the play of the late afternoon light patterning a wall in shadow-stenciled leaves, or fail to examine the woodwork detail on the posts of the stair rail, finding out the origin or date and intent of its construction. We just don't seem to see with the same sensitive eyes as those who do pause to bring their inner selves out into the world in a visible form.

In his book *The Old Way of Seeing*, architect Jonathan Hale states: "Before the machine age, no one had to make the choice to be conscious of pattern, to be aesthetic. Now, to be in visual touch requires taking a deliberate step. Numbness is today offered all around. We fall into it easily. We do have to choose to be awake as people in the past did not."

To have an aesthetic sense simply means to be perceptive, or to take notice of what is going on around us in the physical world and within us where our spirit lives. We have been focusing, so far, on the aesthetics or perceptions of the spirit: our beliefs, values, goals, and dreams. We have been looking inward, observing the architecture of our souls. We have noticed the inner foundation—our beliefs, the walls—values that define us, and the windows providing a view to our dreams. And since

we have experienced what an inspiring place it is, we want to bring the inside to the outside, expressing these inner attributes beautifully with objects, colors, and patterns.

a wake-up call

It took thirty-eight years for Rod Parks to express himself in an outward visual form. His aesthetic eye had enjoyed a nice long snooze until one day when the alarm clock finally went off:

I had never really paid attention to my house before—what was in it. It was a weird combination of bachelor stuff: leftover things from my girlfriend and odd pieces that people had given me. One day I was at an estate sale; I saw this sofa, and I was attracted to it. It was a 1950s armless style with this sculptural shape. It seemed really cool. Now, "seemed" is the operative word here. I was just so unsure of myself, I didn't trust my judgment. I circled this thing a million times and paced back and forth; I couldn't make up my mind if it was a good piece or if I just had really bad taste. Finally, another woman showed interest in it—validating my instincts. I bought it only seconds before she made an offer on it.

As a Ph.D. candidate in psychology, Rod had been living cloistered in an ivory tower of scientific thought. When that first sofa gave his physical senses a resounding wake-up call, they came back to life with thirty-eight years of stored energy. He said:

When I was in graduate school, I would only use sick

A 1960s frosted pitcher with blue ellipses was the objet d'art that inspired stenciled walls in Rod Parks's kitchen. Objects, such as this pitcher, were the impetus for Rod's transformation from numbness for his surroundings to aesthetic awareness. Now Rod's instincts are so strong they've proven marketable. He owns and operates the innovative Retro Inferno Furniture.

days to write papers. With my new passion for furniture, I only used sick days to go to estate sales. The competition at the sales can be fierce. To get in the door early I have had to do many things, including sleep all night in my van, then push, run, jump, and dive through the mob once the doors opened to get what I want.

We may wonder what sort of obsession, addiction, or religious zeal would compel such actions. Rod's description of his quest contains a bit of each with a little romance thrown in:

The first piece I really fell in love and had an emotional relationship with was a desk designed by George Nelson. I still have it and love sitting at it and just opening the drawers and admiring the rationality of the design. It is very "form follows function." It is scientific, which is where the psychologist in me gets expressed. But I find modern furniture also very spiritual. Many people would disagree with that because it is machine made; it's the underlying forms and shapes, though, that are transcendent. The design provides the spiritual suggestion instead of how it was made. It is this genius of my favorite modern furniture designers—such as Charles and Ray Eames, Mies Van der Rohe, Erro Saarinen, Le Corbusier, and Edward Wormley—that I find inspiring. They have all contributed to history with their creations.

Rod's instincts are so good, they have proven marketable. With only four years of experience, he now owns and operates Retro Inferno, one of the finest twentieth-century modern-furniture stores in the country, specializing in designer furniture from the 1930s to the 1970s. What about the Ph.D.? It seems that the gratification of satiating his aesthetic eye has overridden his need for intellectual challenge. Rod left the doctoral program just short of completion to chase his new love— modern furniture. But he had to once again call

upon a little scientific methodology to shape his unwieldy collection into a pleasing composition within his home. The art of bringing it all together had, as yet, evaded him. He said:

I do well with furniture and art objects because I can see them. I can see the good lines, shapes, or colors. But when it comes to imagining a whole setting without seeing it, I don't really know that I can do that. I am very reactionary, I must first see it and then respond. Then I know if it feels right to me. It makes it really hard for me to create a whole setting that will look good. I have just had this ever-changing collection of things I like in a non-atmosphere.

To create a visually beautiful setting requires no art degree or previous experience with traditional concepts of interior design. Nor does it require familiarity with color theory, perspective, or other academic approaches to drawing or painting. We don't need to paint a canvas or a wall. In fact, the less we know about formal art and design, the better. It is all the easier to hear the artistic intuition of our own spirits.

artistic intuition

Ann Aho is an eighty-eight-year-old woman who sees like an artist. She has no training in home decorating but allows her mind's eye to help express her spirit within her home. She must rely on this artistic intuition because she has been blind for the past ten years. Her daughter, Joan Ryan, says:

My mother has the most extraordinary sight within herself. Over the years, she has developed an array of senses that has made her sensitive to things we assume one must see conventionally. The rituals of home decorating that are so important to those who are sighted are still important to her, and, beyond

Previous page: Artistic intuition: Back in the master bedroom, three paintings from Rod's collection of eighty Stewart Claire works are the focal point of the fireplace area. The paintings, based upon Claire's theories of color, were important influences in Rod's own artistic awakening. "I have intuitively made color choices for my home that are in line with the colors in his work. There has been no conscious effort about it," he said. Recently he has begun to study color and often references the collection of paintings.

Left: Watercolor sketches of jazz musicians represent a love of music, particularly the riffs of the Modern Jazz Quartet. A vast record collection stored close by and a rare wire-mesh chair and table by the artist Sol Bloom make a cool corner for listening.

that, she demonstrates how powerful the ritual of belief is through her enthusiastic participation in decorating projects.

At Christmastime, for example, there is a wreath on her door that she selects each year, based on its fragrance and color and size of the bow. She is very particular about whether there are holly berries or pinecones adorning it. Throughout her home, there are baskets of potpourri and branches of fir and pine because the fragrance means Christmas to her. She has a small Christmas tree with carefully selected ornaments that all have special meaning to her, and, even when she is alone and cannot see the bright lights, she will turn them on because she loves the vision in her mind's eye.

There are many other times when I am struck by her ability to "see." When I help her select her attire for a special occasion, she will want to know precisely which dress I have chosen, what color it is, does it have flowers in the pattern, is it long or short, and then she will excitedly decide whether she should wear her strand of pearls or a locket. Each time, regardless of how many times she has made that same decision, she is thrilled with this creative act and ritual, just as she was the first time.

On Mother's Day, she is surrounded with flowers and other gifts from her ten children, grandchildren, and great-grandchildren. Each gift is given a special place on a mantel, dresser top, or table, and she instructs others on how to arrange the flowers or hang the plaques and photos with their loving messages.

We are spiritually sensitive beings occupying a physical body in a physical world. Our deepest impulses stir us to phrase the meaningful associations we hold dear into more permanent statements that we can visually experience again and again. We want to bring out the uncontainable joy of the human experience—love, revelations,

friendship, family, and traditions—where we can see them. If visual affirmations of our likes and loves weren't important, someone like Ann would not cherish them so. In that virtual studio of our inner sight, the inspiration of the heart is organized into artistic scenes of amazing composition and radiant color.

inner sight

Giving way to the longing of the creative spirit within, many people set out to make a home that truly feels like their own. But lacking experience and a working philosophy, they become disillusioned. Dazed and neck deep in fabric swatches and paint samples, it appears that those artistic impulses were deceptive, leaving many hopeful but without the artistic experience to pull it off, so some place an emergency call to an interior designer. Yet others proceed forward into the land of the promised living room—the all-in-one decorating center. But when the reality sets in, this is a very artificial idea of a home, laboratory-perfect coded into sets with matching artwork designed for instant shake-and-bake perfection.

The reason so many well-intentioned people settle for prepackaged decorating is simply that they lack understanding of some basic artistic premises. The simple concepts to which I refer are deeply imbedded ideas about color and pattern that are, in fact, present within the inner sight of everyone. One of my clients used to constantly refer to herself as "artistically impaired," but her kind of blindness had to do with a perceived lack of inner sight.

Even though we can doubt our capacity for artistic thoughts, we have undeniable proof that we do indeed have an inner sight. This proof can be found in our dreams. As we rest the physical body, for example, our subconscious creates colorful dramas within the theater of our imagination. While sleeping we narrate great stories and paint beautiful scenes. When we are uninhibited by waking fears and distractions, the creative spirit flows smoothly, showing its artistic ability. Some say this is a good model of how our best artistry comes about. "You don't create the work, you step out of the way and let it happen" is a popular adage of artists. Those who are artistically expressive have learned to use this power of the imagination in their waking lives: seeing the world through the twenty-twenty vision of their inner sight.

Artists and great thinkers are often referred to as visionaries. That is precisely what they are, and that is the secret of their power. They have used their imagination to see their creations in the mind. From our historical vantage point the great works of art may seem like the work of seers, people quite unlike ourselves. They are shrouded in mystique; their art just seems to happen. We are in

awe, and without an understanding of how such work is created, the process is out of reach. However, before the great painter Henri Matisse ever laid down a single brush stroke toward the completion of one of his beloved interior-setting paintings, he had vision and an understanding of a few artistic premises. By examining his way with color and pattern, we can begin to understand how to paint our own houses of belief into an outer representation of our own inner vision.

the Matisse method

Mindy wanted something more but didn't know how to get it. "If I see another manufactured-looking room with all the coordinated accessories, I am just going to lose it!" she said, throwing the magazine on the hill of already discarded design periodicals we had perused. Just out of law school, she had no trouble speaking directly while making dramatic gestures. "There is just no real-life there! I need a free feeling and spontaneous space—give me another magazine."

We continued on with the fact-finding exercise, in which she looked for pictures of rooms that had a certain visual and visceral appeal to her. This is the next step after the foundation work of identifying inner concepts, beliefs,

Left and opposite: The gold-leaf diamond pattern of a vintage coffee carafe inspired a wall design in the master bedroom. Favorite collectibles, from dishes to textiles, suggest wall colors and patterns throughout Rod's house.

Page 79: The hub/wheel concept: In the living room, a modern stained-glass sculpture became the hub of color inspiration for the entire house. Colors extracted from the piece fanned out to the kitchen, dining room, and master bedroom like spokes from the center of a wheel. Colorful accessories repeat the color scheme throughout Rod's home.

A sofa compact designed in 1954 by Charles and Ray Eames provides high-design seating in the living room. A space-age Ericofon from the same period makes for vintage conversation.

values, goals, and dreams. The idea is to find physical elements that create color combinations with resonance, furniture styles, and aspects of light and space.

"Oh, wait now . . . I love that painting," Mindy said, pointing to a print by Henri Matisse. "That is what I want my home to look like. It makes sense, because I have always loved Matisse . . . the colors . . . especially the still-life paintings . . . guess what? I even have a postcard of one in my book of belief!" Why not, I suggest, do a room devoted to her love of the artist and his paintings? It would be like living inside one of his canvases. And given his mastery of the use of color and pattern, it would be a course of study with the master himself; she could use the eloquent strategies of composition he painted on canvas in creating her room.

The idea I envisioned was not to match everything to the painting and then hang a print of the painting at the center of it; that would be too close to the classic couch-painting offense of buying the artwork to match the furniture. However, this idea of actually copying the room setting from a Matisse still life is not unlike the painting exercises used in art schools in which students are asked to copy the work of masters. In fact, I have hanging in my own kitchen a very fine art-school copy of a Paul Gauguin work. The masters themselves have historically looked to the work of other artists before them for inspiration. This process Mindy would engage in of using the Matisse in this way would actually flatter the painter, as he himself constructed interior designs later in his life.

If we want to begin to see like an artist, an artist is the best one to teach us how to do so. In the same way that Geraldine Lloyd helped us to understand the more meaningful and symbolic

side of belief-based decorating in chapter two, we can learn aesthetic points from Henri Matisse.

still life with geraniums

After giving much thought to which Matisse painting she would like to walk into, Mindy selected his 1910 oil called *Still Life with Geraniums*. "This relaxed and slightly rustic atmosphere is the way I want my bedroom and the attached sun porch to feel. Right now work is chaotic and I need a place to ground myself and get a little peace. To me this painting looks peaceful."

Because she was single and just out of school, budget was an important consideration for her. So she decided to try to make most of the things in the room herself, even though she didn't have much experience at it. To get her started, I asked her to study the painting and make an illustrated list of the patterns and shapes she found in it.

Next she identified the colors—very specifically. Instead of just calling the painted wainscoting or paneling in the scene lavender, she looked into its peculiarities, noting that the general appearance was lavender but the grooves in the wood were deep blue, the highlights white, and the general color was truly a blue-lavender. These details would later help her in creating the right color in the room.

She did the same for the other hues in the painting. She found color chips at a paint store and matched them directly to the painting; then she fixed them into groups next to the color description. For example, in the still life, a table radiates red but on closer inspection is really a combination of color patches—orange, cherry, rust, and gold—that visually blur into the vibrant red the eye perceives.

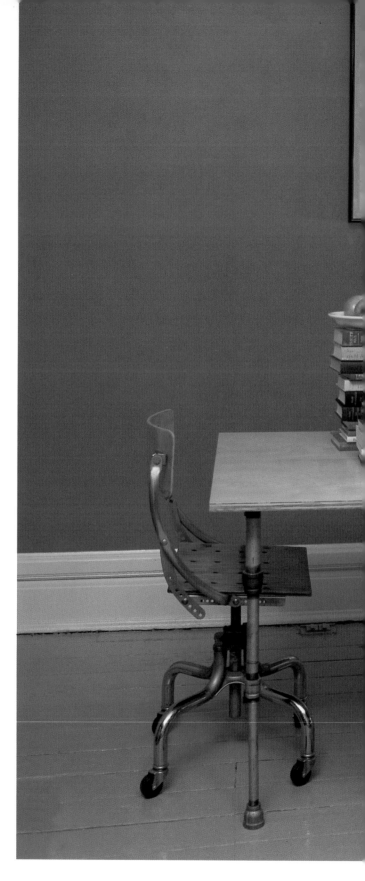

With these two rituals of belief completed, we met over lunch for another discussion. That day she brought photos of the room so we could start applying the painterly techniques of Matisse to her home environment. I also suggested that she do a hub-wheel diagram and a thumbnail sketch to aid in her visualization of the room.

In this concept, an inspirational hub, which can be an artwork, an area rug, or a fabric, is used as a starting place for the overall visual approach of the room. Mindy's Matisse painting is the hubcap, or center, of a wheel. It contains most of the colors and patterns to be used in the space. Spokes fan out from the wheel, which represent individual colors or patterns taken from the painting. At the outer end of each spoke is the intended application of each color or pattern. For example, according to her diagram, she used the pink and red geranium blooms from the painting as a pattern to stencil on her chair cushions.

Right: Laura and Andy Rowzee, who reupholster furniture by trade, didn't blink when the mind's eye presented a different vision; they left the fabric off these roller chairs. Using raw pipe and a choice piece of maple plywood, they created a dining/library table to match. Andy's mind's-eye painting watches over all, sees all.

Above: The entry hall of Laura and Andy Rowzee's 1880s townhouse—with its ten-foot ceilings and long walls—offers gallery space for Andy's paintings. The matching bookshelves take on a bookend appeal when placed on either side of a vintage chair.

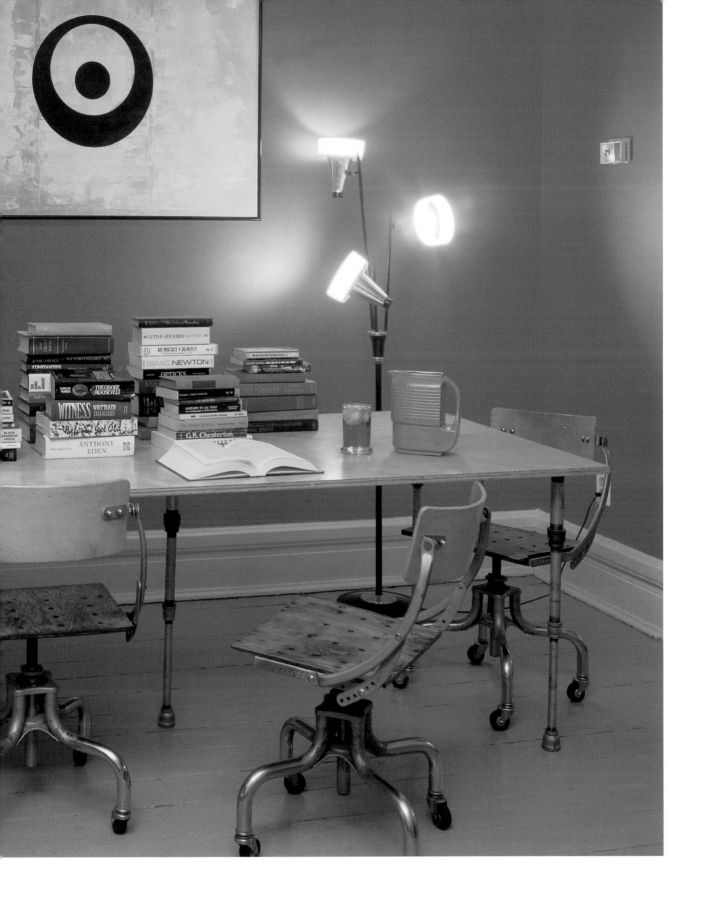

Right: Kitchen redux: This time Laura tried her hand at painting directly on the curtains for the doors and windows. Some acrylic fabric paint was brushed onto cotton fabric. A metallic spray paint was applied to an out-moded refrigerator to give it a hammered-steel finish.

Above: A stainless-steel colander was reassigned to the role of a light fixture.

Left: Two people, one vision: In the couple's kitchen, Laura free-painted a lampshade in a style similar to Andy's abstract canvases. "It is uncanny how closely we see things," she says, "we rarely disagree on aesthetics."

Above: Painted primitive squiggles adorn the clever pulls on the Rowzees' pine cabinets.

the hub-wheel diagram

The hub wheel is a tool to help you visualize your own unique ideas. For Mindy, the rationality of the diagram was very comforting to her pragmatic attorney's mind. She could see and, therefore, understand how it all would work in balance and harmony. Remember, seeing is believing; the diagram helped her to believe in her own ideas. This mildly scientific approach also made great sense to Rod Parks, the modern-furniture collector, in creating a whole house plan that would accommodate his diverse collection of art and furniture.

I suggested that Rod begin with items he had selected intuitively, looking to their colors and patterns for assistance. It so happened that at the very hub of his house—in the central living room—one of his most prized pieces, a massive modern stained-glass window, was already displayed. Contained within the glass were all of Rod's favorite colors: chartreuse, tangerine, crimson, turquoise, and lemon. The window became positioned at the center of the diagram. Colors extracted from the window would fan throughout the house, coloring various rooms.

For further embellishment of the space he looked to the color and patterns of other art objects he had selected intuitively: a frosted-glass carafe with blue ellipses spotting it and the wild geometry of a painting by Stewart Clare. By using the hub diagram, both Rod and Mindy were able to plan the flow of visually beautiful spaces inspired by that which they loved.

the unveiling

Because Mindy wanted to see her way through this project by herself, I vowed not to visit her home until she felt she had accomplished her goal. She really needed the emotional safety of privacy to allow herself the opportunity to learn to see like an artist and make her own mistakes like one, too.

Finally, about eight months after our first meetings together, Mindy invited me to see her "walk-in-painting."

Entering the bedroom, my eye was immediately drawn to the opposite wall with its French door opening to the sun porch. The doorway made the perfect frame for the setting. My heart sped up with delight. It was midmorning and the eastern light highlighted the blue-lavender walls, making a chroma-keyed backdrop for a small picnic table, freshly painted in orange-red with an illusory swath of blue arabesque fabric painted right on the top of the table. She had chosen to whimsically interpret the fabric drape from the Matisse in a trompe l'oeil.

Two 1930s metal porch chairs in rusty copper brought the patina of age to the setting, while ready-made canvas cushions in rose pink, embellished by Mindy's geranium stencils, update them with comfort. Between them was a small table with a lamp in the shape of the Eiffel Tower she had found at a discount store. On the cotton Roman window shades Mindy used a fabric paint marker to write all of the titles of her favorite Matisse paintings. She said this helps her mind's eye to conjure up visions of them. On the concrete underfoot, she painted sienna-gold floorboards defined with red pinstriped grooves, referring to the wood floor in the painting.

Stacks of art books and decorative painting-technique manuals, as well as paintbrushes—pleasingly arranged in her grandmother's antique Hull vase—provided physical evidence of the young attorney's creative unveiling.

Like any student with his or her teacher, Mindy stood by, holding her breath and self-consciously examining her paint-stained fingers as she awaited my response. And she got it—my most congratulatory statement—a warm hug!

"Only through art can we get outside of ourselves and know another's view of the universe, which is not the same as ours, and see landscapes of the moon. Thanks to art, instead of seeing a single world, our own, we see it multiply until we have before us as many worlds as there are original artists."

—Marcel Proust

Mindy and Matisse: how-to highlights

1. Make a Gold File: As a fact-finding exercise, find pictures of interior settings that have visual or visceral appeal to you. Collect and keep these pictures in a folder and create a gold file of your favorite influences. They can be any aspect of a room or whole house—from wall treatments to furniture styles. In Mindy's case, all she could find was a Matisse print included in a room photo, but it was enough. It reminded her of her love for Matisse. Even though she had a postcard of one of his still-life paintings in her book of belief, she didn't make the connection between it and the way she wanted a whole room to feel until we did the Gold File exercise. Look for the following as you search:

- ◆ Color combinations
- ◆ Wall finishes
- ◆ Pattern uses
- ◆ Fabric applications
- ◆ Furniture periods and origins
- ◆ Wood finishes
- ◆ Floor treatments
- ◆ Cultural influences
- ◆ Lighting
- ◆ Architectural details
- ◆ Art and collectibles

2. Use Mindy's Process:

- ◆ Select a painting
- ◆ Make a pattern list
- ◆ Create a color chart
- ◆ Draw a hub diagram

Even if you are not taking this approach for creating an actual room, it is a valuable exercise to be worked out on paper. This is a good time to begin to use your art supplies, particularly the markers and colored pencils you acquired when bringing together all of the right atmospheric elements for your creative greenhouse in the preceding chapter.

a ritual of belief

Select one color and one pattern from your favorite painting or art object. Find a way to incorporate these into your home. For example, you may find a pattern from a painting or a fabric. You can use the pattern any way you like—from walls to windows. Choose from Mindy's applications or create your own:

- ◆ Paint a wall or floor.
- ◆ Write titles or messages on fabric (for example, window shades, tablecloths, or pillows).
- ◆ Stencil a pattern on walls, fabric, or furniture.

Use your watercolor art markers and colored pencils to do a few simple planning drawings so you can work out your idea before you begin. If you are working with wall- or floor-paint techniques, try out the mixed paint colors ahead of time. The greatest success comes when we spend a little time preplanning before each creative activity. Remember that even Picasso had to try many times before he got the results he wanted.

one home, two dreams

Once awakened, the mind's eye likes to see things its own way; compose its own artistic vision. Complications can arise when there is only one home but two separate visions. Over the years I have worked with many couples in their homes, endeavoring to start them on a lifelong process of belief-based home decorating. I always require that both parties participate in the process. At times, I have been very successful, inspiring them to use the canvas of their home to express themselves individually and together in creative ways. Many couples report positive side benefits, better communication, a revitalized love life, and a deeper and more spiritual connection.

At other times, I have found myself hunkering down as if in a foxhole in the middle of a World War III conflict. Each new subject—from the merits of flowers versus stripes,

Above: Laura and Andy added legs to a chessboard and refurbished two has-been chairs to great effect. Like most artists, they couldn't resist a signature, ROWZEE, written with black-and-white monogram pillows.

Opposite: Hip and handmade, Laura and Andy Rowzee's moderne drawing room was inspired by favorite objects and experiences, including a trip to New York City, a friend's drawing of ancient Athens, and the popular movie 2001: A Space Odyssey. A futuristic black-and-white floor pattern and H.A.L, painting refer to the movie. Floor-to-ceiling curtains hang in Greek columns and hotel-style furniture from the 1960s and '70s make home into a Big Apple vacation.

Left: A ritual of belief: the Rowzees computer scan images of people who have influenced them in their creation of a belief-based wall hanging. The framework is a wood grill that can be purchased at any home improvement center.

the relevance of a mother-in-law's china cabinet, to whether a nail can be driven into a newly plastered wall to hang a picture—becomes an emotional bomb buried just under the hardwood floors.

Rarely, though, is the conflict about what it seems. All physical elements have a subjective meaning, some associated idea that is unique to each person. The reason submerged tensions explode when it comes to discussing the home is that these meanings are often unclear to the person who holds them; they lurk in the subconscious. If we can't identify why we despise the antique china cabinet, then how will our partners accept our views as being important and meaningful to us, choosing to honor these views in deference to our feelings? Only when we are capable of deciphering the personal significance of objects can we begin to communicate them to our partners. When our significant other has an understanding of how a particular decorative element represents something about our inner self—beliefs, values, goals, and dreams—we have a foundation for sympathetic communication that can lead to shared creativity and actions of belief-based home decorating.

step one
celebrate your sameness

It is easy to get fixated on points of difference. But focusing on your differences will get you nowhere. It's time to compromise. Whether you as a couple are just beginning to create a house of belief together or are already over your head in differences, recalling what actually brought you together instead of focusing on what divides you will ease the ensuing tension and recenter you in the consciousness of the agreements that bind you. Think back to the day you realized you were destined for one another. How did you know it was right? Light a few candles, pour some wine, put on some soft music, and use the following questionnaire to prompt your romantic memories.

1. What first attracted you to one another?

   a) Physical attributes?
   b) Style?
   c) Humor?
   d) Charisma?

2. What are some of the first evidences of sameness you experienced?

   a) Where did it happen?
   b) What brought up the point?

3. What was the sameness?

   a) A favorite movie, song, or book?
   b) A childhood experience?
   c) A dream or occupational goal for life?
   d) A travel destination?
   e) A love of the same painting at a gallery exposition?
   f) Family?

4. Recall a wonderful day spent together.

   a) Why was it memorable?

5. What is your favorite shared activity?

   a) Cooking?
   b) Hiking?
   c) Building?
   d) Artistry and craftsmanship?
   e) Reading?
   f) Architecture?
   g) Concerts?
   h) Antiquing?

6. What is your shared philosophy for your relationship?

   a) What beliefs brought you together?
   b) Values?
   c) Goals?
   d) Dreams?

This exercise needn't be comprehensive. It is just an introductory conversation that will help to refocus you on why the two of you fell in love. The next step is for you to part company—only temporarily—and begin an independent journey of discovery and recovery of forgotten concepts. Only when we understand how to relate our inner concepts to the physical realm of our homes can we successfully do so with another.

exercising the concepts

Now is the time to focus on yourself independently. The answers you cultivated in step one are probably those that come to mind easily. But there is so much more to be remembered.

Independently work through this text—chapters one through seven, including the exercises. All exercises and rituals of belief should be done privately; do not discuss your answers or ritual results with your partner—not yet, anyway.

When you have completed this work individually, you can then proceed to contrast and compare your results with your partner. You will find many more points of sameness, and you will find some differences.

WARNING: Avoid jumping to dire conclusions. At this point, abstain from making any final judgments. Many times, that which looks like a difference on the surface can actually have similar underlying meanings to a preference of your own.

artistic differences

What, you may ask, are the results when two people, whose life vision and creative ideas become compatible, find that they have different working styles? They can celebrate their spiritual sameness but can't lift a paintbrush together without a mortal conflict. Consider artisans Laura and Andy Rowzee; together they share a slipcover and upholstery business. Also, Andy is a successful canvas painter. At first they were not unlike many couples who express differences in methodology and problem solving. But Laura and Andy have succeeded in finding an operating procedure that has preserved their romance and made their business prosper. Here is how they do it:

♦ Divide tasks; do not attempt to do the same task. For example: Laura cuts and sews while Andy applies the fabric to furniture.

♦ Do not expect your partner to work at your pace. Set a general deadline for each activity; allow each to govern his or her own time.

♦ Keep large-scale work out of the living space. Andy and Laura's workroom is in the basement. They leave their creative disagreements behind in the shop.

ritual of belief: a life affirmation

Bring together your shared beliefs, values, goals, and dreams into a life affirmation. You may write it yourself or find a famous literary quote or spiritual affirmation that you feel represents you. This statement will serve as a constant reminder of all that you represent together. Then you may choose to use the entire statement or only a part of it, perhaps drawing out a specific value such as friendship, for example, that you would like to perpetuate on the walls of your home or on furniture or fabrics.

One couple found a quote by Whitman—"The ornaments of a house are the friends who frequent it"—and stencil-painted it upon their fireplace mantel. This simple phrase announces the open warmth of their hearts to all who pass over their threshold.

Andy and Laura Rowzee began by listing those people throughout history who had lived inspiring or meaningful lives. Next they found images of those listed via the Internet, encyclopedia, and biographical books. Each image was photocopied or scanned and then mounted within the frames of a wooden window grill purchased at a home-center store. The result is a stunning wall hanging that is the focal point of their living room.

A final couple who was to be married chose to embellish a wedding chest with the names of great creative soul mates, mythic and real: Simone de Beauvoir and Jean-Paul Sartre, Georgia O'Keefe and Alfred Steiglitz, Marie and Pierre Curie, among others. They simply generated the words from a computer and then découpaged them to the chest.

In their bedroom, Laura and Andy once again shared the artistry. Laura sewed the blue-velvet bed fittings, while Andy wielded the paintbrush. Together they created a faux stained-glass window by utilizing an old door and spray paint for the glass.

the *look* of belief

the individuality of objects

The following story of my grandmother Mary, named "Maema" by me when I was a child, illustrates the significance of sacred objects in home decorating. Maema handcrafted beaded Easter eggs every year, one for each grandchild.

Opposite: Lee and Jackie Frickey made conscious connections, matching their personal ideals with period style elements that would best embody them. The couple's personal integrity is strongly indicated in the gleam of their eighteenth-century furniture craftsmanship, dressmaker curtains, trompe l'oeil painting techniques, and the architecture of the colonial house itself.

Above: In the drawing room, ball-gown-like curtains, with the elegance of Jackie herself, clothe the windows.

She wore vibrant silk scarves wrapped around her head like a mantle of eccentric creativity. As I made a remembrance list in which I listed objects of sentiment, these two vivid images—eggs and scarves—came to mind.

Maema had a number of husbands and boyfriends. During a love affair, she wore her clothing with fashion-doyenne effect. She had many costumes, each designed to entertain. As a finishing wrapper to the eccentric package, Maema would swath her head in silk or chiffon. What began as a practical defense for her coiffure against the wind could look for all the world like a gypsy halo.

Maema worked in a greeting-card factory, which had one sparkling benefit: glitter. Because many of the greeting cards in those days had glitter applied to them, there was always a surplus available. After awhile it became her fairy dust, capable of

Opposite: A historical event: Calligrapher Michael Sull, who has penned many documents for United States presidents, was asked to apply the Frickey family history to the wall in the entry of their home. The story begins behind the portraits of great-great grandparents and continues in a family book.

Right: Individuality of objects: Lee's love of architecture and family heritage are on display in the entry hall. A carved Palladian gazebo and antique family portraits, with their history written in calligraphy directly upon the wall, form an interactive gallery of belief. Bronze stars painted over an aged federal blue wall glaze, as well as flag-striped portiere curtains, play up the character of the colonial structure.

enchanting her with thoughts of a new kind of creativity. Jars of glitter lined her cupboard like magic powders on a gypsy's cart. They were capable of magic, too, shifting a round Styrofoam form into a dazzling Faberge-style creation. Using her fairy dust, pearls, beads, lace, rickrack, and sequins, she lovingly and carefully embellished her eggs of belief.

As a devout Roman Catholic, Easter was an important holiday for her. On Easter Saturday (between Good Friday and Sunday), it was a tradition for our family to go with Maema to an afternoon

mass to have the food she prepared—eggs, polish sausage, and assorted breads—blessed by a priest. Following the service we would go back to her house to feast on the blessed food and to receive one more evidence of Maema's sacred belief: a glittering Easter egg.

The Easter egg, a particularly evocative image of new life, represents the Christian holy day well. It shows up in many other cultural traditions, too, a symbol of developing potential and promising good things in the hatching. Perhaps Maema intuited this significance, choosing the egg as her image of a new life of artistic expression.

As a ritual of belief, Maema's egg-making worked to renew her creative spirit. While creating, she glowed with that in-love kind of radiance. The artistic outlet seemed to fulfill her in the same way romantic relationships had done and more. She exhibited a new sense of self-worth during these times, and love flowed from her heart. The furrows softened, and the darkness lifted. When I look at and hold Maema's gilded eggs, I am reminded of the necessity of creative expression for a love-filled life. And though she has been gone for many years now, I am grateful to still have her fairy-dusted embryos of love and creativity.

sacred objects

The story of Maema helps to illustrate how an object—a personally sacred object, like one of her gilded eggs—can tell an illuminating story. Until I made the list and considered those holiday objects

Curtains with the detail of eighteenth-century gowns adorn the windows. To create the elegant draping, pulleys similar to those used in antique hoopskirts were sewn into the lining.

that are meaningful to me, I had never really understood the significance of this creative activity in my grandmother's life, nor had I truly comprehended why I cherished the eggs so much. Each little egg does physically represent her more ethereal attributes of spirit, the glittering potential of the woman herself.

The things our lives are made of speak a silent narrative of who we really are or aren't. So far, we have focused on identifying our inner concepts and then finding images to represent them. In the assessment of this holiday ornament, I used a reverse process. I started with an object for which I had a sentimental feeling, although I wasn't sure what the feeling was trying to tell me. Through a process of memory, association, and deduction, I was able to arrive at the true meaning of the feelings I had about the little eggs, leading me to establish a new and expanded sense of life values.

the individuality of objects

Emotions are the inner structure keeping a belief intact. When we cease to experience the emotions associated with a belief, that belief is at risk of crumbling. This is the reason a house of belief must evoke feelings. We say, "I am feeling emotional." This statement indicates the relationship between our feelings and our emotions.

Just as the appearance of special possessions such as Maema's eggs evoke strong positive feelings within us, so can the objects from which our homes are made. We can consciously use the look of a thing to evoke the feelings we want to affirm, comfort, or motivate us. In this manner, we intentionally use the elements of our homes—architecture, furniture, fabrics, colors, souvenirs,

In a powerful collaborative ritual of belief, the Frickeys commissioned an artist to reproduce Caravaggio's fruit basket still life for the hearth kitchen. Crewelwork curtains accented with buttons from the West Indies add to the colonial feeling.

heirlooms, handcrafts, and more—to infuse our lives with empowering symbolism.

To become conscious of meaning today, especially in home decorating, requires some effort because the look of our homes has become disassociated from the feelings of our spirits. The design-industry's accepted approach to achieving a look is that the sum is greater than the parts. For example, a French-country look might require yards of paisley, stuffed roosters, and curvy-legged, pickled-pine furniture. Taken individually, these items may not have great personal significance or appeal, so they just become part of a package, intended to fulfill the specifications of the look. It is this kind of style-oriented decorating that has

numbed our senses to the individuality of objects. The object has become separated from its spirit, much in the same way we have.

We can see the thing—a chair perhaps—and identify it only in terms of its function or superficial meaning. A wing chair is only valued for its physical comfort or appropriateness to the style. We have forgotten that grandfather was a successful banker and had a chair like it behind his desk. Reviving these feelings, the chair now connotes success, strength, and power, fall days spent with grandfather.

A chair can be much more than a chair. In a passage from Anthony Trollope's *Barchester Towers* a manservant describes Mr. Plomacy's appreciation of a special chair:

His moments of truest happiness were spent in a huge armchair in the warmest corner of Mrs. Greenacre's beautifully clean front kitchen. 'Twas there that the inner man dissolved itself, and poured forth streams of pleasant chat; 'twas there that he was respected and yet at ease; 'twas there and perhaps only there, that he could unburden himself from the ceremonies of life . . .

Mr. Plomacy's armchair became his place of spiritual transformation. It became an outer image that promoted inner happiness. Sitting in the chair was a ritual that helped Mr. Plomacy reconnect with himself.

Of the better-known chairs in recent history, the well-worn recliner of Archie Bunker from the sitcom *All in the Family* is now enshrined in the Smithsonian Institution. As the archetype of old-fashioned male stoicism and bias, this 1970s recliner stands as a symbol of a certain kind of man.

Clearly, not all associated meanings that we find in the objects around us are good ones. A material form such as a chair can stir up unre-solved conflicts or unpleasant memories. One of my clients complained of extreme anxiety at holiday times. After doing a careful assessment of the objects in her home, we found one silent enemy: a harmless-looking child-size rocker that sat to the left of her fireplace mantel. The rocker had been a childhood possession of hers, a Christmas gift from seasons past. She began to think about the circumstances surrounding the little chair and described her memories to me:

Our house was a boiling pot at Christmas time. My mother would get more and more frantic as the day got closer, and my father would drink a lot. By the time Christmas Day came, my brothers and I were in dread. There would always be a big fight. The year I got my rocker was really bad; my father left and didn't come back for days.

The vision of the rocking chair subconsciously degraded her ability to believe in the goodness of the holiday season, hindering her chance for healing. After she became aware of the subliminal message the rocker was sending her, she decided to put it away.

the crystal chandelier

Belief-based home decorating is the conscious creation and display of material objects to support and express our spiritual or authentic self. Just as out of sight is out of mind, in sight is in mind—and heart.

Our homes become an interactive gallery of all that we are and aspire to be. By surrounding ourselves with the trappings of our past successes or things we associate with those who have achieved the success we want in our lives, we begin to believe in the possibility of our dreams. Here is the story of how two clients have done just that.

As a schoolboy growing up on a farm in western Kansas, Lee Frickey hadn't had much exposure to the world outside his small town. For Lee, the future looked as flat and uneventful as the Kansas landscape until a drafting class he took in high school populated his mind with high points; he became interested in skyscrapers and buildings. In fact, he became so skilled in drawing and rendering that he won a university scholarship to study architecture.

But instead of pursuing that dream, he pursued another one and married his high-school love, Jackie. Over the years the two of them raised a family and created and managed their own small businesses that grew into a national company. They prospered, becoming sort of a poster family for the American dream. In the midst of managing his responsibilities as a husband and father, architecture wasn't uppermost in Lee's mind. However, the artist within him maintained a keen architect's eye. When the Frickeys decided to buy a suitable home, his intuitive sense of design and architecture was reawakened.

Some thirty years after he first studied it, Lee was once again contemplating the merits of the classical orders of architecture. There was much to think about: Greek columns and pedi-

ments, iron ornamentation, period-style construction techniques, and the suitability of the style of the structure to match his and Jackie's beliefs and dreams. Here was an opportunity for Lee the architect to gain a mode of expression.

The Frickeys chose a grand brick colonial, a house that would act as a constant symbol to them of their commitment to the American dream. This columned and pedimented early-American home—with its organized features, balance, and proportion—is a visual affirmation of security and success.

Lee's interest in architecture and the Frickey sense of family heritage are the values that guide their artistic expression throughout the house. A Williamsburg-style clock tower has been hand painted over the mantel, and a hand-carved miniature Palladian gazebo is the highlight of the entry foyer; both announce Lee's passion for architecture. Farther down the main corridor, family heirloom portraits are centered over the hand-painted calligraphy story of Great-great-grandmother and -grandfather Frickey.

Above: Dream imagery: The Frickeys' cut-crystal chandelier is the focal point of their dining room. The vision of this crystal chandelier represented a belief that the their youthful dreams had, indeed, become fulfilled. The light of the chandelier reflects not only on the mirror but also off an antique, silver soup tureen.

Left: Quality statements: In this formal dining room, eighteenth-century-style furniture with fine detailing—inlaid dovetail joints and intricate hand carving—bespeak the Frickeys' values.

Following page: This furniture design ritual of belief references historic periods of furniture for inspiration. Select or create furniture designs that reflect your beliefs and values, just as the Frickeys have done.

The story has been painted directly on the wall in a style of faded Jeffersonian penmanship. Federal stars punctuate the deep blue walls, forming a historic border pattern near the ceiling.

In the dining room and drawing room, the coral and maize-gold walls are colored as softly as antique linen; they have been glazed and aged to imply the passage of time and a respect for the wisdom of experience. The furniture is handmade in the tradition of Chippendale, Hepplewhite, and Duncan Phyfe. The curtains have been crafted with the elegant details of an eighteenth-century ball gown.

Every detail in the Frickeys' house is representative of some aspect of their own character. In business they believe in quality and craftsmanship; their home is handcrafted, embodying that ethic. They love and value their family; family heritage is perpetuated in the wall motifs; Lee's interest in architecture is evident in the clock tower, gazebo, and architectural renderings; and Jackie's love of old-world artistry is apparent in the period details of paint and curtains.

Jackie tells me there is one special detail that has had particular emotional significance for Lee:

One evening I noticed Lee out in front of the house on the sidewalk. It wasn't long after we had completed the renovations and had put everything in place. It had just grown dark, and he paced up and down the street in front of the house, occasionally stopping and looking back at it. This went on for a couple of hours. When he finally came in, he had an odd expression on his face. I asked him what he had been doing, and he said he was looking at our new crystal chandelier through the windows. I was so touched, I nearly cried. I remembered when we were young, back home in Ellis, we used to drive by the grand old houses and admire them, especially the crys-

Scale

tal chandeliers that could be seen through the windows at night. That crystal chandelier really makes us feel our journey . . . and success.

the look of belief

The vision, or look, of the Frickeys' crystal chandelier physically represented their belief in the fulfillment of their dreams. Dreams can be a crystal ray in the proverbial night of hard times; it's as if the light became as real as the dream. And, poetically enough, even the house, in its architectural vernacular, embodies a 200-year-old dream—the American dream. In selecting the structure, Lee and Jackie made conscious connections, matching their ideals with a period style that would best reflect it.

The value they place on quality and integrity in materials and construction can be seen in the gleam of mahogany furniture with old-world craftsman details—inlaid bandings, dovetail corner joints, and hand-rubbed finishes. The dressmaker curtains clothe the windows with the elegance and grace of Jackie Frickey herself, so she is ever present within the room, and Lee's feeling for family heritage is written out on the calligraphy wall.

The Frickeys have done an admirable job in executing a thoroughly belief-based expression of home decorating, even incorporating the architecture of the house into their belief concepts. For others to do the same with as much success will require following some of the same fact-finding exercises that they followed. The process described on the next page can help any person find the true meaning within objects, clothing, and furniture, and then begin to find physical elements that make his or her feelings resonate.

exercising the concepts: egg and chair

Objects stir up feelings within us. Feelings are the language of intuition, and intuition is the very spirit within us. So feelings are actually communications from our spirit. A spirituality expert on the *Oprah Winfrey Show* repeatedly asked an audience member what she was feeling inside. The poor woman, teary-eyed and confused, said she couldn't distinguish her feelings from her thoughts. That woman is representative of many of us. Sometimes it is hard to distinguish the intellectual thoughts of our minds, what seems right, or what others view as right for us. Many distractions add to our confusion; life is so loud and hectic that we can hardly hear the quiet whisperings from within, telling us the truth of what we feel. That is why we need physical images to remind us, to help us feel again. This process of memory, association, and deduction will help us to use objects of sentiment and the furnishings of our homes to uncover what we feel and to perpetuate the best of those feelings.

egg

Review the holiday objects of sentiment you listed in a previous chapter. Select one. Objects that have been either handmade or given to you by another will provide the best information and tell the most profound story. Bring the object out of storage right now. Put it in a prominent place. Meditate upon it. Ponder these questions:

1. What memories do you have about the circumstances in which you received it?

a) Who gave it to you?

b) What were their motivations? Was it handmade and from what materials?

c) What are the gift-givers like personally?

d) What was the holiday like that year— food, guests, gifts, rituals?

2. What associations do you now have with the object?

a) How do you feel when you recall these circumstances?

b) Do you feel the image of the object is empowering?

c) What feelings do you value most highly and would like to perpetuate?

3. What deductions or knowledge can you draw from contemplating the previous questions about the object?

a) Do you now understand more about the person who gave you the object and your relationship than you did before?

b) Is the object a good symbol for you to use in the future?

c) What do you believe the feelings associated with this object mean?

d) How can you use this information in the future?

a ritual of belief: holiday object

During the holidays, feelings run deeply. It is an appropriate time to become more aware of what those feelings are saying and, also, to begin to create your own rituals and objects to help you evoke the feelings you desire. Remember that feelings are the supporting structure of belief. So it follows that by evoking feelings, you also help to sustain or build belief.

One workshop participant, Jodi Collins, created her own ritual of belief in conjunction with Mother's Day. She describes the process she went through.

When I got married and had children, I thought my marriage would be forever, but it wasn't. This past year I was divorced. I felt that as a mother I had really messed things up, dirtied my life—and my children's. Mother's Day brought up these feelings of failure. So on Mother's Day I began to search for a symbol to represent the way I felt about the dirty condition of my life. I thought dirty . . . dirty . . . what's dirty? Then I saw plates in my sink. Yes, a plate can be dirty—or clean! I brought my two girls into the kitchen and pulled three plates out of the cabinet. I explained to them that as a mother I felt I had failed them and had dirtied our plates. But now I would like to start over with clean plates intentionally filled with all of the good things we want in our lives. I then invited them to use the porcelain paint I had on hand—to paint the things they wanted in their lives in the next year—and I would do the same. Jessica made a shiny sun and wrote "joy" and "love" on hers; Alexis sketched a house and "God"; I wrote "family" and "wisdom."

Here are the steps to follow in creating your own ritual of belief:

1) Decide upon the goal of your ritual, the idea you would like to express.

2) Choose a symbol or object that represents the idea.

3) Decide what creative actions you will take to transform the object.

4) Act out your ritual of belief. With full focus and consciousness transform the object, allowing the change to occur in your spirit as it happens to the physical object.

chair

Mr. Plomacy's armchair provided him with a means to reconnect with himself. Lee and Jackie Frickey's handmade furniture, curtains, and crystal chandelier helped them express the value they place on quality, integrity, and hard work. What does the furniture in your home represent to you? What does the furniture that you would like to have symbolize? Once again, work through the process. Start by selecting one piece of furniture you currently possess and one you would like to either create or acquire.

1. What memories do you have about the pieces you currently have? Answer each question for each piece.

a) Is it old or new? What is its function?

b) Is it an heirloom or acquired antique? What are the materials, color, and finish of the piece?

c) Was it handmade or embellished by you?

2. What associations do you have with the piece?

a) Did you acquire it on a trip? Where?

b) What historic period or style connotation does it have? Do you have a connection with that period of time or the culture in which it originated?

c) Is the piece from someone in your family? What do you remember about that person?

3. What deductions can you make about the piece?

a) If the piece was handmade, is it more meaningful?

b) Would you like to create your own furniture?

c) Could the culture or origin of the piece be a meaningful style direction for you? Do you value this style of art, architecture, beliefs, ideals, ethics, and general personality?

a ritual of belief: furniture
the meaning of style

As we discussed earlier, mimicking a popular style is a spiritually hollow proposition, like the French-country look—complete with meaningless objects that fulfill the style requirement. However, historic periods of style can be used to advantage when they match your particular value set. In the Frickey story, we find this point well illustrated. The key is to find style elements with which you resonate on an inner level. In the last chapter, we created a Gold File and collected magazine pictures and images of furniture and interior elements that had a purely visual or tactile appeal. Now, refer back to that file and look for deeper meanings in the style of the elements. In considering a French-influenced concept—or any other—consider pertinent questions like these that will help you deduce whether the style offers you anything meaningful:

If the style is French, do you like France—its people, customs, ways? Would you like to live there? If so, then owning French-provincial furniture is a powerful visual affirmation of your love of the culture and dream of living there. The important thing is to make sure that the furniture you use is not sending you a derogatory message or making you feel ill at ease in your own kingdom.

Refer to your book of belief for more clues as to meaningful influences. For example, you may have stated that Italy is a place you would like to visit because you love opera and wine. Then research Italian decorative arts, architecture, holidays, traditions, and history. Also, peruse travel guides. Look for colors, motifs, clothing, furniture, or anything else that takes your fancy. Visit the Italian section in your bookstore or library and see what you can turn up; it will feel like a mini-vacation—I promise!

Above: Trompe l'oeil paint techniques transformed a storage area in the drawing room to a limestone wall niche.

Left: In the Frickeys' living room a Williamsburg-style clock tower has been hand painted over the mantel. The furniture is handmade in the style of Chippendale, Hepplewhite, and Duncan Phyfe. Camelback damask sofas were codesigned by Lee and Jackie.

creative
partnerships
building a community house of belief

No doubt about it, shared actions of creativity can bring people closer together. In Victorian times and before, group creative activities formed the backbone of the community and offered individuals the chance to share in creative expression.

Opposite: A creative partnership between the author, Habitat homeowners, and artist Tammy Smith produced a colorful wall mosaic that encourages all to believe and create. The phrase became the group motto for the House of Belief workshop series. Participants came to believe in their own creativity, empowering them to make the window coverings, furnishings, and other amenities that they need for their Habitat homes.

Above: The first Habitat House of Belief, in Kansas City, Missouri, was formerly a broken-down drug house. The exterior displays Caribbean colors, a palm-tree porch rail, and beach landscaping as a visual affirmation of the participants' dreams of exotic travel.

Sewing bees and barn-raising picnics are a good example of this. In reviving a sense of community today, this grass-roots approach is once again proving successful. In fact, Habitat for Humanity International helps low-income people build their own homes through the old-fashioned activity of barn raising—a community house-building effort.

When I approached Winston Slider, the executive director of Habitat for Humanity in my hometown, he enthusiastically embraced my desire to volunteer my talents to Habitat. I proposed to donate two years of my time to develop a House of Belief program that would focus on the inside of the Habitat home. The main goal for Habitat up until this point had been simply to put shelter over needy heads; there was no interior aspect. Many residents are single moms who have had life struggles but who are really trying to make a better life

Artistic miracles: A fireplace mantel became a working fountain; a crude concrete floor was painted with rock shards and inspiring poetry; castoff wooden two-by-fours were turned into a primitive blue wainscoting; three-dollar thrift-store shutters were refinished for the window; a sisal carpet remnant was painted in bold Caribbean stripes; raw canvas was stamped and painted with personal symbols for the sofa and chairs; and a throw-away lamp was rewired to light up the whole setting.

for themselves and their families: working two jobs, studying to get a GED, and caring for and supporting several children is difficult. So, many residents are without window coverings or furniture in their Habitat homes. Living in a house barren of the essentials, I have been told, has had a spiritually debilitating effect. And, without belief in themselves and in their own creativity, they have no way to acquire the costly items that would enhance their homes.

As a former director of Habitat's work in Africa, Winston said that he truly understood the need for such hands-on creativity because he had witnessed the spiritually renewing effects of artistic expression there. And, he said, something was missing here in America, a sort of disconnection from that inherent sense of creativity seen as natural in the African cultures.

He went on to share with me a few examples of the creative resourcefulness that he had seen there. First, there was a market day when he was on his way to a medium-sized village and saw a tribal woman making her way up a steep bank. She had approximately fifty pounds of produce piled into a hand-woven basket balanced on her head. Dressed in batik fabrics imprinted with her own symbols, she also carried a baby on her back. As he got closer, he could see the irregular movement of her gait, caused by her leaning heavily upon a hand-carved walking stick. It became apparent that she was missing one of her legs. Yet, she likely had grown her own food, woven the basket, made her clothing, carved the walking stick, raised the baby, and was successfully making her way to market. She was creatively powerful; she could make whatever she needed.

Another individual who was without both of his legs made hand sandals so that he might hand-

walk over the rough terrain. He also was very skilled at making rubber stamps by carving old tires with such detail that letterheads, addresses, and business cards could be printed with computer-font accuracy. These may seem like extreme cases, but they do represent the creative resourcefulness that characterizes the continent.

The craft of home-building as fostered by Habitat and its founders Millard and Linda Fuller, whose mission is to help provide shelter for God's people in need, was cause for community celebration upon completion of a home in Africa. Winston recalled one home dedication:

The street swelled with thousands of people singing, dancing, and praising the Creator. It went on for hours, and just when the energy seemed to be dissipating, it would start up again. The act of building a home in Africa in collaboration with your community is looked upon as a ritual that forges relationships with God and with one another.

Winston sadly said that he has never witnessed anything even close to this here in America; but it is Habitat's goal around the world to build homes and communities.

I explained to Winston that belief-based home building and decorating could help to solve both of these problems. Residents could learn to make their own window coverings and to revive and transform their old furniture or thrift-store finds and begin to create a true home inside and out for themselves and their children. And as they looked about their homes at the things that they made with their own hands, they would have physical proof that they are creative. They would begin to believe in themselves. Then they would wonder, If I can do this, if I can make these things, what else can I do? Maybe get a college degree, or open my own business, or even . . .

Right: Self-reliance: Habitat home-owner Janice Busbee sewed her first pair of curtains and embellished them with a twenty-five-cent-per-yard ball fringe. Also, a garage-sale Hawaiian shirt was cut into a tropical valance for the window. Hand-painted pillows displaying interests, such as this one illustrating music, were made by workshop participants. They are economical (approximately five dollars each) as well as meaningful.

Above: This attractive hand-painted pillow is another creative project made by the House of Belief residents.

Love is the passionate dance between two hearts. It is to believe in the dream, and together make it real.

Sylvana Rosetti

Right: The workshop participants decided to view the bedroom as the ultimate cocoon, or place of metamorphosis, with the image of a butterfly in full three-foot glory painted by Phyllis Harris above the bed. Butterfly images were also stamped onto the linens and the roller shade at the window. Habitat homeowner Angie Cage painted the gold-star centerpiece pillow, and the faux iron bed was created from PVC pipe by the workshop participants and artist Evadene Judge.

Following page: What is your dream? The House of Belief kitchen illustrates the dreams of workshop participants Gloria Hamilton and Rosalind Malone to own restaurants. The handmade mosaic backsplash announces "Soul food is food for the soul." Each tile represents a Habitat homeowner's favorite food. Artist Tammy Smith led the project.

With visions of a future American Habitat community celebration to rival that of the joyous African one Winston related, we made plans to launch the first House of Belief program for Habitat for Humanity. We would begin with a twelve-week Habitat-community workshop series based on this book. I would lead the group, assisted by ten artists, to help with teaching various techniques: Claudia Cooper, stamping and book making; Jackie Denning, painted and printed fabrics; Tammy Smith, ceramic and mosaic art; Mike Savage, canvas painting; Sonya Nicholson, furniture and wall painting; Evadene Judge, mixed media; Steven Haack, mural painting; Phyllis Harris, stamping and decorative painting; Jamie Kelty, assemblage and children's art; Laura and Andy Rowzee, upholstery; and Ken Mc-Whorter, upholstery. The series would culminate with the creation of a community House of Belief, a whole house artistically decorated with many beliefs, values, goals, and dreams of the Habitat residents—truly a joyous celebration.

finding belief

At a recent House of Belief meeting, Habitat resident Winnie stood up to share the contents of her Book of Belief with the workshop group:

On the cover, I have a picture of a face; it represents my mind. Then as I open my book, I envision opening my mind, and inside are my thoughts that are sacred. I found this quote by John Milton, it says, "Tis nothing good or bad, but thinking makes it so . . ." Sometimes I have trouble with negative thoughts, and I have suffered from depression. I have created symbols here in my book to represent how I feel. First, there is a box; sometimes my self-esteem is so low, I feel like I am in a box and can't get out. Then there is a squiggly line for my courage because it is high and low. This pyramid represents my faith; when I leave the box and call upon my courage, I am able to climb to the top of this pyramid.

Sharing our Books of Belief and other creative projects with one another proved to be a heart-opening experience, helping us to authentically connect with each other. We began to see that, truly, deep in our hearts we all feel the same. Despite our outward differences—racial, economic, or occupational—we feel much alike.

Next, Ladedra shared a page in her book on which she had fixed a picture of her small daughter with a note beside it:

My little girl was doing very badly at school. Since I am by myself, I have a hard time raising my children at times. I didn't know what to do. The teacher called everyday. One night I just broke down and prayed, asking God to help my daughter and me. The next day when she came home, she had this note that said, "Much better!" I will never forget that and put it in my Book of Belief because to me this note looks like a miracle. I believe in miracles

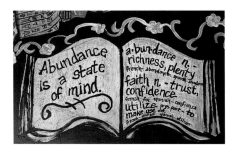

Above: As indicated on this table detail, abundance is truly a state of mind.

Right: Artist Sonya Nicholson and the workshop participants brightened up standard Habitat budget cabinets with an orange and red stain. Some door panels were removed and grooved glass was added for a diner feel. Salvaged bathtub drains were transformed to back plates for the drawer pulls. The vintage appliances were donated.

Opposite: Month-of-belief calendar: This wall-sized chalkboard keeps a record of the positive events of life. The most uplifting event is recorded each day; by the end of the month there will be at least twenty-eight reasons to believe.

Table of Abundance: A salvaged schoolhouse table was painted by artist Jackie Denning with witty images and phrases of abundance, such as "My cup is half full," "Ask and receive," "The world is my oyster," "Mucho Dinero," and more.

when I look at it, and I don't forget what happened. It is like an affirmation.

After a workshop on fabric painting for upholstery and curtains was taught, Janice Busbee shared a valance she made from fabric and stencil-painted with empowering symbols:

I have used the image of a hand as a symbol to represent my goals. I want to make a living from working in artistry and craftsmanship with my own hands. When I was about seven years old, I decided I wanted to be a fashion designer. I just started sewing and was

really good at it. My father told me that I was stupid and that I could never make a living at it. I held on to the dream for many years, but as a teenager I had heard him say it so many times that I finally gave up. I started getting into really big trouble then and my life has been constant problems ever since I gave up my love of sewing and fashion. So my goal is to leave the specimens-processing lab where I work and open my own alterations and custom clothing shop.

Some participants, though, didn't take to the concepts so easily. Doretta is one of them. Never missing a session, she would sit sullen, arms

Above: To the workshop question "What do you want on your plate?" participants responded by painting plates with symbols and words in answer.

Opposite: A built-in seating area, detailed with corrugated aluminum, features seats that lift for storage.

crossed, and skeptical. When I emphasized that all of us are creative, that we just need to find our niche, she would shake her head in disbelief. For many weeks she never completed a ritual or project. Yet she never missed a workshop. Finally, one day she showed up with her Book of Belief. She shared it with me privately and explained that while everyone else was so family-oriented, with pictures of parents in their books, she didn't have any . . . because she had been raised in an orphanage. She didn't believe she had abilities.

That same day, as if by divine providence, Sonya Brown, a keystone of the group, shared a poetic writing of her own she had included in her Book of Belief. It spoke to Doretta and the rest of us. It is called "Exploring You."

As knowledge hasn't yet introduced you
to chemistry or construction of the Taj Mahal,
nor have you ever developed an empire
*   or spoken*
with the eloquence of a King or Queen,
perhaps an original invention hasn't entered
your heart or mind, nor have you exercised
your power to create a multitude of followers
*   for a common belief,*
or you haven't the opportunity to perform
in a motion picture where your face is
*   known over*
the world from place to place. Inject a sigh
*   of relief,*
for it was not yet the time.

Fathom this: It is according to time and belief.
Today let time permit belief to enter the
    kingdom of your soul,
transforming your mind, electrifying your
    thoughts,
and graphically developing your dreams.

Concentrate on your Creator who has formed
    you to perform a
very important role upon life's journey,
    knowing that no
matter what, your dream will be released into
    this reality.

building a house of belief

This heart-and-hands workshop process that employs the various creative rituals found in this book to identify and then physically express our beliefs, values, goals, and dreams became the blueprint from which we created our community House of Belief and from which the participants built and decorated their own homes. A home that has been built with this kind of conscious intent as to its meaning becomes an empowering visual affirmation of all that we believe in. The potential to experience such empowerment is the opportunity that Habitat residents have ahead of them and that all people who begin anew through the ritual of belief of building one's own home can aspire toward.

Not always, though, can we start over with a brand new house. That was the case with the community House of Belief our group was to make. We had inherited an old drug house, and the house's body and spirit were in the expected state of sadness. The physical body of the house told the whole story poetically, too, for its very foundation had

crumbled. The windows were darkened, boarded over, keeping light from finding its way inside. There were rooms laden with refuse—clothing, furniture, keepsakes, family photos—and even a dog was left to die in the place, all representative of cast-off values, beliefs, and dreams. Anything or anyone could lay claim to the space—the doors had been left open; the interior was vulnerable and exposed.

Opposite: Artist Mike Savage led workshop participants in painting a mural of their ideal Habitat community.

Left: A painting by Habitat homeowner Tamiko Brooks was heat-transferred to this footstool.

Above: A canvas slipcover was embellished with fringe inspired by the African technique of pitchy-patchy.

Opposite: In the Habitat children's room, African cultural heritage is represented with a map of Africa painted directly upon the floor. A growth chart stamped onto the bed rails will tell any child how many zebras he or she is in length. Written on the sheets by Habitat teen Ebony Byers are answers to the question "What makes you feel safe?"

Above: Habitat grandchild Julian takes his turn on a winner's platform created from a salvaged milk crate.

Left: Resourcefulness: A sheet of butcher's paper stamped with animals and a curtain rod finished with toy zebras make an economical window treatment. A thrift-store desk repainted by workshop participants and a throw-away cabinet remade by artist Jamie Kelty are resourceful solutions for anyone.

But, for both houses and people, it is never too late. Our group gathered up positive ideas like cornerstones to shore up the foundation. Beliefs in equality, honor, integrity, family, human potential, and God were reinstated. The plaster walls were embedded with the values that define us: love, strength, courage, patience, creativity, partnership, and understanding. Soon the house's window-eyes cleared of negative perceptions; the view became peopled by those who had inspired us. The interior visually affirmed dreams of travel, love partners, college degrees, artistic pursuits, creative careers, healthy and happy children, and more. Now no undesirable thing can pass through the doorway of this rock-solid fortress of belief.

the art of transformation

As the Habitat residents transformed the old house, they saw that they do have the power to transform their whole lives. Humble, even homely, materials became a thing of beauty: tree branches took shape as a frame for family photos; old bedsheets painted with one's own story turned into window coverings; secondhand furniture took on a new life through paint and mosaic tile. Something old became something new. Something crude became something elegant in both appearance and meaning. Through this process of belief-based decorating, nothing seemed beyond transformation—negative thoughts, financial trouble, loneliness, nothing.

It becomes so easy to believe in ourselves when we have firsthand proof that we are creative. We see that we have participated in a miracle, transforming raw ideas and physical materials into evidence that the Creator is within us. A common property of miracles is this ability to see them. And when we saw them, we began to believe.

Those first small creative miracles within our homes will lead us to much larger actions of belief in all of life. It works the same for everyone. If we are creative, we are powerful. We can always create a way to accomplish what we want, need, or dream of—from home and family to finances and career.

Below: Residents drew this symbolic column into a wall in the House of Belief.

Following left page 130: Women-who-believed window shade: Inspiring women from many cultures adorn this unique roller shade.

Following right page 131, top: Month-of-belief calendar: Thinking positively—at least one uplifting event a day is written here.

Following right page 131, bottom: Freedom-to-create chair: Habitat homeowner Darlene Parker created this ritual of belief to help her let go of limiting ideas.

a ritual of belief

true-colors paint jars

The color scheme for the living room was formed from the answers to the workshop question: If you could name a color to describe you other than the color of your skin, what would it be and why? The question helps us to think beyond the limiting cultural definition of our skin color. Some of the paint colors chosen were put into the creativity cabinet in the living room for further use in projects. They were labeled with the picture of the resident they represent. To do the same, simply photocopy a picture onto transparency paper. Cut out and use rubber cement to fix in place.

fabrics of life

For economy and meaning, the residents painted and hand-stamped their own fabrics. For one to three dollars per yard, patterns were created featuring their own innovative color combinations. This striped fabric was made by applying two-inch masking tape to a lime-colored linen fabric. Turquoise acrylic paint was brushed in the alternating stripes, then the masking tape was removed.

symbolic columns

To represent the residents holding up the walls of the House of Belief, their personal symbols were drawn onto the walls. Using a wall-texturizing plaster, draw in the symbols that best state a belief or value. Create your own signs and symbols, or do as Habitat residents did and call upon the West African Ashanti symbolic language. There is a small tree to represent family abundance, a dove for Christian faith. Our convergence of creative energy is conveyed through the Ashanti knot. An African heart motif proves to be the universal symbol for love. A geometric windmill means strength among the winds, and a chain image hints that our lives are all interrelated.

women-who-believed window shade

This window-shade idea is taken from Habitat homeowner Sonja Brown's Book of Belief and features images of inspiring women from many cultures: Toni Morrison, Marion Anderson, Isadora Duncan, Indira Ghandi, Zora Neale Hurston, Sarah Winnemucka, and more. The images are photocopied and then applied to the shade using a spray adhesive.

ritual of belief:
form a house of belief group

Belief-based home decorating is an activity that empowers individuals and forges relationships. House of Belief workshop participants exchange creative talents; cultivate positive beliefs, values, goals and dreams; and generally build community spirit and cooperation. Your own House of Belief Group can do the same. Organize a meeting of people you know who have creative and artistic talents or those who would like to have. A group size of eight to ten members works well.

Work through this book together; take a chapter per week. Meetings should allow a minimum of an hour and a half in length.

When you have met a few times and feel comfortable with your group, select a group leader who will really commit to learning and applying the concepts—someone who is already aware of, and in touch with, the creative

month-of-belief calendar

In a conscious choice to celebrate the positive events of life, this wall-sized chalkboard is meant to keep a daily record. By the end of the month there will be a visual affirmation of at least twenty-eight positive occurrences—something to celebrate. Chalkboard by the foot can be purchased to cover a wall, door, or table. Simply use an interior adhesive to fix in place.

freedom-to-create chair

Habitat Homeowner Darlene Brenson-Parker had struggled with issues of limitation her whole life. Her elderly grandmother had been a slave, and Darlene had felt the oppression she suffered. Needing an action to accompany the change of mind and heart she endeavored to make, Darlene gathered together her materials. Using a garage-sale chair, cut-out images of Abraham Lincoln, pennies, and computer-generated words, she made a ritual of belief designed to set free her own creative spirit.

belief-based home-decorating showhouse for/with them. Be sure to involve their residents directly.

As areas of interest and specialty arise in the group, be sure to exchange your talents with one another. When we invest in each other's homes, we invest in each other's lives.

For further information about organizing a House of Belief group or becoming certified to create your own House of Belief Community House, please call or write to:

House of Belief, Inc.
3520 Central Studio 3-N
Kansas City, MO 64111
(816) 931-3496

To contact House of Belief artisans or find out about seminars near you, visit our Web site at: www.House of Belief.org

spirit within. She or he will bring experience and insight to the leadership position.

Spend thirty minutes discussing the belief-based home-decorating concepts. Answer any questions that come up from the chapter reading. Then, allow another thirty minutes for sharing the results of the exercises or rituals you did at home the previous week: for example, the Book of Belief.

Take the next hour for a hands-on creative activity or ritual of belief. You may also create your own rituals and supply the materials accordingly. Guest artists are wonderful at demonstrating a particular technique. For example, invite a paper- or book-making artist to lead the Book of Belief ritual. Or, invite a fabric artist to lead the fabrics-of-life ritual.

Remember to plan a group project to help someone in your community through belief-based home decorating. After familiarizing yourselves with Habitat for Humanity, if possible, take a field trip to a Habitat project site or other shelter-oriented agency. Offer to create a House of Belief: a

Making a room for creativity: workshop participants wanted to create a living-room space that nurtured creative pursuits for the whole family. Space was made for art, music, reading, conversation, study, and prayer or meditation. This creativity cabinet was fashioned from a fifteen-dollar thrift-store hutch and filled with plenty of supplies, including stamps, paint, buttons, yarn, pencils, markers, secondhand beads, and dried leaves.

profiles

In the salon room, Steven Haack, a painter and muralist, helped to bring the author's belief-based allegory to life. Working together over a year, the two referenced science texts, historic manuscripts, and literature. Steven says he enjoys helping to bring his clients' meaningful ideas into the form of paintings and murals.

To work on her illustrated journals, cancer survivor Geraldine Lloyd chooses the nurturing comfort of her bedroom in Frederick, Maryland. However, the artist now spends much of her time in Key West, Florida. "I received an arts endowment there to work on a group of large-scale paintings illustrating spiritual concepts. They will be included in a mixed-media public presentation," she said.

The young actress Adair Moran continues to work on her craft. She recently completed a study trip to England and has signed a contract to become a player in an ongoing production in her hometown. "Acting is my life," she says.

Cathi Horton's imagination is now drawing an even bigger picture, expressing her creativity on a new canvas—corporate America. Her company, appropriately named Imagination Studio, is revolutionizing the workplace with more creative team-building concepts, including variety shows, videos, and conference planning. Scooby the tomcat acts as her office manager.

Earth mother Claudia Cooper isn't happy unless she is sharing her natural creativity with the children she teaches. She says that someday she hopes to open a school that makes developing and nurturing creativity a priority. She also continues to entertain and share her cultural heritage through performances in which she sings, plays her guitar, and tells ethnic myths and stories.

Rod Parks is now entering the third year of business for Retro Inferno, his twentieth-century modern-furniture store in Kansas City, Missouri. And he continues his love affair with high design: he recently purchased a second home that he describes as being architecturally cutting edge. "My furniture looks sculptural in the minimalist environment," he says.

Laura Rowzee's artistry is lately receiving great applause. Her slip-covers, which display meticulous sewn details, are being featured in national magazines. The former attorney says she's much happier since she and husband, Andy, have opened their own upholstery and slipcover business. "I am glad to be free of the constant conflict of legal work," she said.

Besides sharing an upholstery business with his wife, Laura, Andy Rowzee is a gifted canvas painter. Andy says that Laura is his muse. Her encouragement helped him to overcome his reluctance to paint. Now his works are a major feature of the couple's belief-based decorating; Andy often paints into reality an idea the couple formulated together. The couple share their house of belief with their dog, Magnus, a 150-pound mastiff.

Maema's creativity seemed to always be at work—whether she was making glittering Easter eggs for her grandchildren or making an interesting life for herself. She was beautiful and flamboyant, with gypsy dark hair and big flashing eyes that could adore or just as easily curse. And she had great stories to tell about her coterie of famous friends; she said that she once swam with Johnny Weismueller the original motion picture Tarzan, and she knew the actress Jean Harlow.

Lee and Jackie Frickey continue to build upon their house of belief, adding treasures found in expeditions around the world, the embodiment of memorable times spent together. Because business often leads them to the Orient, the couple has acquired ancient porcelain vases, lacquered cabinets, and paintings.

Jodi Collins and daughters, Jessica and Alexis, use creative rituals of belief to enhance their relationships. "The plate-painting ritual we created on Mother's Day was a very healing experience for us," Jodi says, "and creativity gives us all something in common." She adds that she would recommend creative rituals to all parents as an excellent means of communicating with children.

Gloria Hamilton's dream box became the inspiration for the kitchen theme inside the Habitat House of Belief. And Gloria herself is an inspiration to all she meets. The sixty-five-year-old professional counselor brings a wealth of wisdom and experience to the Habitat project, dispensing advice to the younger women. "Respect yourself," she says, "because it's all you really have."

The Habitat project drew in family and friends to help make the House of Belief a reality. Habitat poet Sonja Brown's son Dante used his calligraphy skills to paint his mother's poem, "Exploring You," into a trompe l'oeil stream upon the floor.

Community volunteer Jerry Van Hooser is representative of many individuals and companies who donated time, products, and services to transform the old drug house. Jerry spent countless hours cutting and fitting wood trim to windows, cabinets, and doorways.

A few of the House of Belief community volunteers, artists, and Habitat homeowners include (front row, seated) Gary Aragon, Gloria Hamilton, Mary Harbin, Pat Gilmore, Tammy Smith, Crystal Shook; (second row) Keisha, Laura and Andy Rowzee, Ruth Webb, Jodi Collins, Mike Savage, Tamiko Brooks, Janice Busbee, Winston Slider, Sonja Brown, Brian Shook, Jackie Denning, Claudia Cooper, Darlene Parker, Phyllis Harris, Ladedra Edwards; (back row) Meisha, Evadene Judge.